E S T A T E   P U B

G000299134

SLOUGH·WINDSOI   D

COOKHAM · FARNHAM COMMON · O   RT

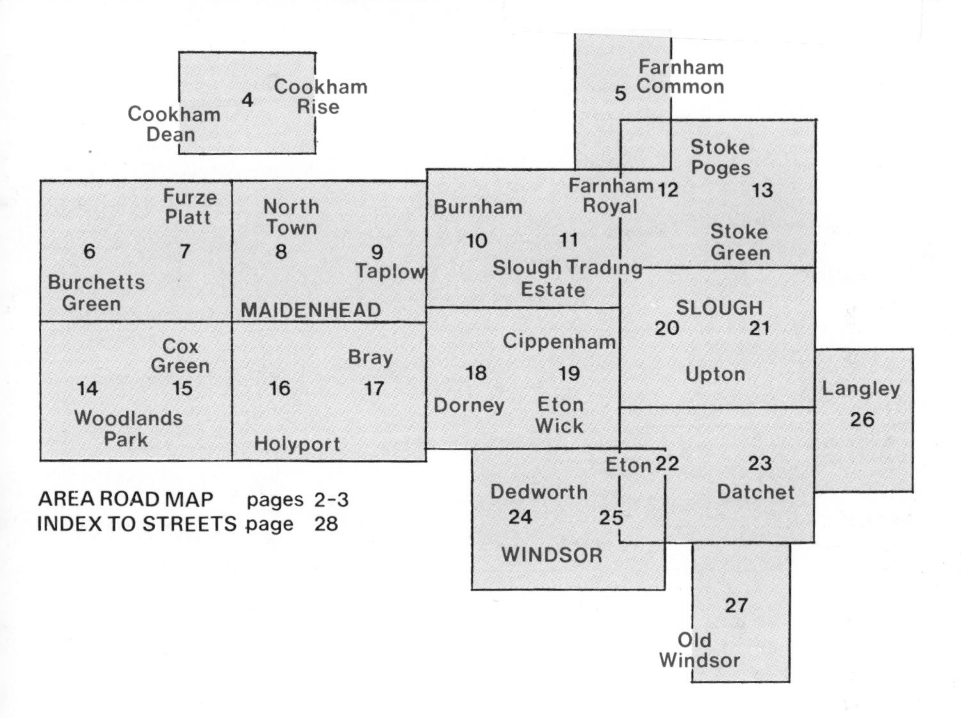

Cookham Dean — Cookham 4 — Cookham Rise

Farnham Common 5

Stoke Poges

Furze Platt — North Town — Burnham — Farnham Royal 12 — 13

6 — 7 — 8 — 9 Taplow — 10 — 11 — Stoke Green

Burchetts Green

Slough Trading Estate

MAIDENHEAD

SLOUGH 20 — 21

Cox Green — Bray — Cippenham

14 — 15 — 16 — 17 — 18 — 19 — Upton — Langley 26

Woodlands Park — Dorney — Eton Wick

Holyport

Eton 22 — 23 Datchet

AREA ROAD MAP   pages 2–3
INDEX TO STREETS page 28

Dedworth 24 — 25

WINDSOR

27

Old Windsor

Every effort has been made to verify the accuracy of information in this book but the publishers cannot accept responsibility for expense or loss caused by an error or omission. Information that will be of assistance to the user of the maps will be welcomed.

The representation on these maps of a road, track or path is no evidence of the existence of a right of way.

Car Park	P
Public Convenience	C
Place of Worship	+
One-way Street	→
Pedestrianized	▨
Post Office	●

**Scale of street plans 4 inches to 1 mile
Unless otherwise stated**

reet plans prepared and published by ESTATE PUBLICATIONS, Bridewell House, TENTERDEN, KENT.
The Publishers acknowledge the co-operation of the local authorities
of towns represented in this atlas.

Ordnance Survey® This product includes mapping data licensed from Ordnance Survey®
with the permission of the Controller of Her Majesty's Stationery Office.

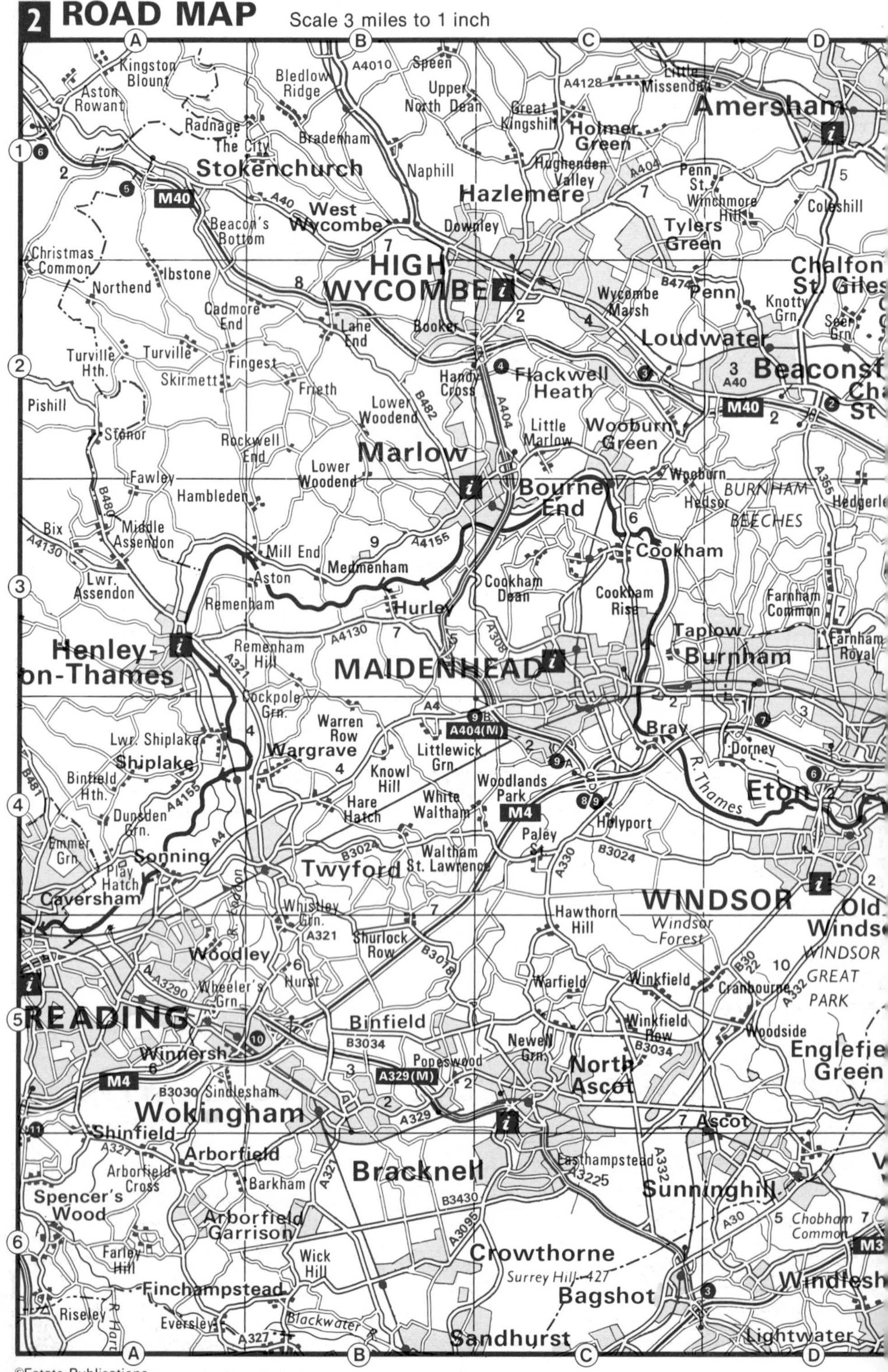

2 ROAD MAP

Scale 3 miles to 1 inch

©Estate Publications

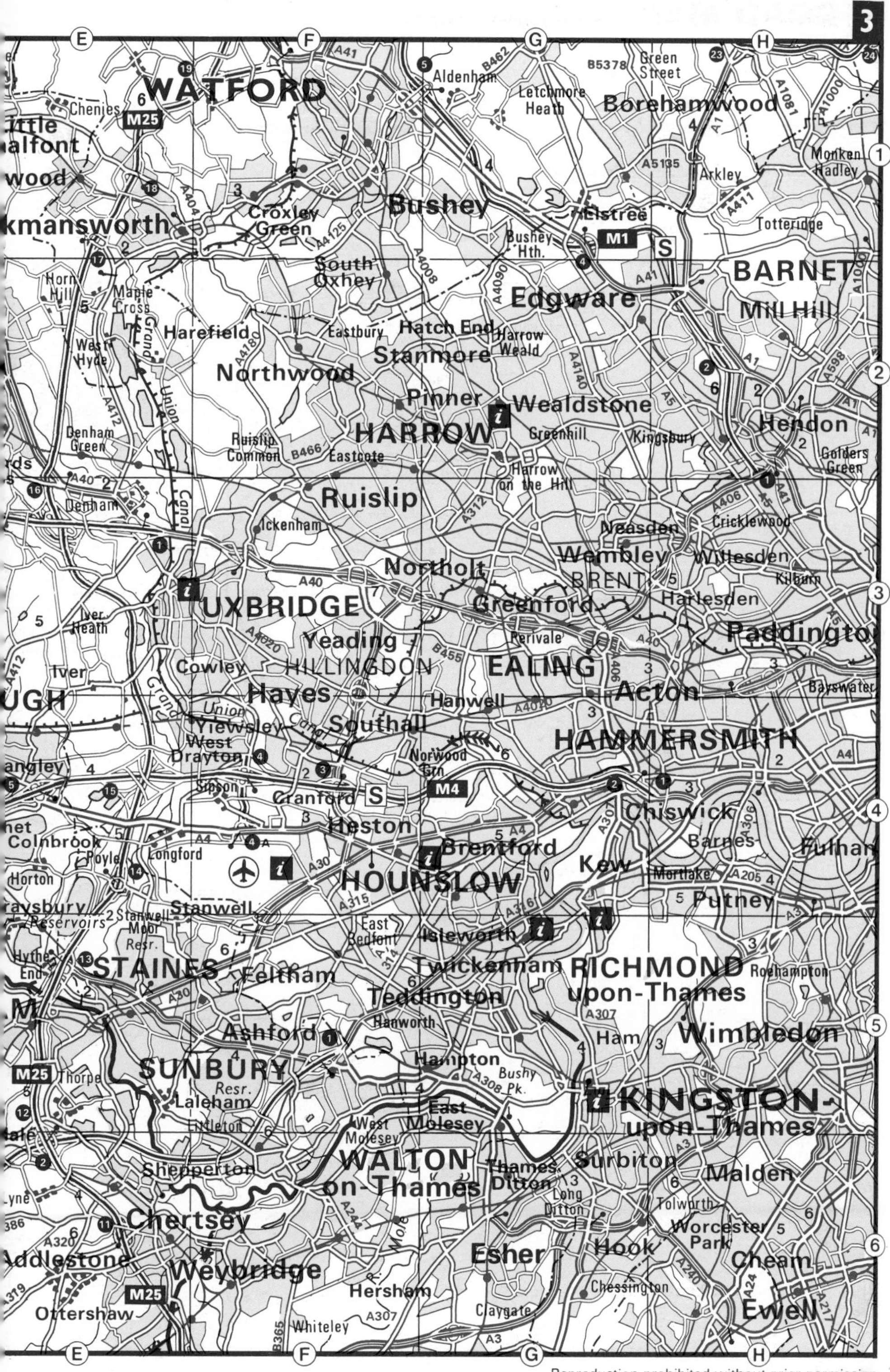
WATFORD
Chenies
M25
Aldenham
Letchmore Heath
Green Street
Borehamwood
Arkley
Monken Hadley
Totteridge
Croxley Green
Bushey
Elstree
Bushey Hth.
M1
South Oxhey
BARNET
Mill Hill
Edgware
Maple Cross
Harefield
Eastbury
Hatch End
Harrow Weald
Stanmore
Northwood
Pinner
Wealdstone
Hendon
HARROW
Greenhill
Kingsbury
Golders Green
Ruislip Common
Eastcote
Harrow on the Hill
Denham Green
Denham
Ruislip
Cricklewood
Ickenham
Neasden
Wembley
Willesden
Northolt
BRENT
Kilburn
UXBRIDGE
Greenford
Harlesden
Iver Heath
Yeading
Perivale
Paddington
Iver
Cowley
HILLINGDON
EALING
Bayswater
Hayes
Hanwell
Acton
Yiewsley
West Drayton
Southall
HAMMERSMITH
Norwood Grn
Sipson
Cranford
M4
Chiswick
Colnbrook
Heston
Poyle
Longford
Brentford
Kew
Barnes
Fulham
Horton
HOUNSLOW
Mortlake
Putney
Stanwell
Stanwell Moor
Resr.
Reservoirs
East Bedfont
Isleworth
STAINES
Feltham
Twickenham
RICHMOND upon-Thames
Roehampton
Teddington
Hanworth
Ashford
Ham
Wimbledon
SUNBURY
Hampton
Bushy Pk.
Thorpe
Laleham
East Molesey
KINGSTON-upon-Thames
Littleton
West Molesey
WALTON on-Thames
Shepperton
Thames Ditton
Surbiton
Malden
Long Ditton
Tolworth
Chertsey
Worcester Park
Addlestone
Weybridge
Esher
Hook
Cheam
Hersham
Chessington
Ottershaw
Whiteley
Claygate
Ewell
Union Canal
Grand Union Canal
Mole

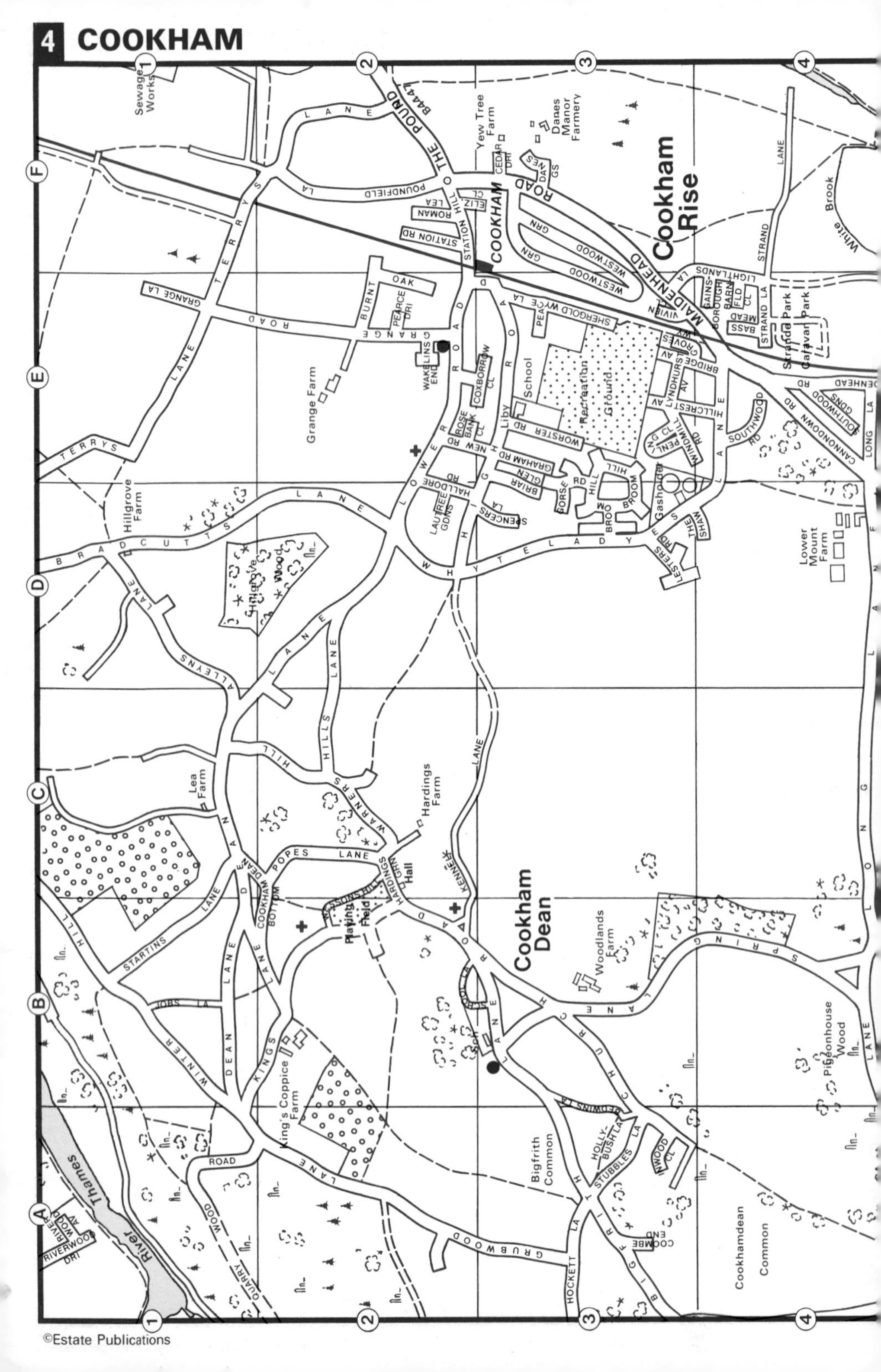
Sewage Works
THE POUND
B4447
POUNDFIELD LA
Yew Tree Farm
Danes Manor Farmery
CEDAR DRI
Cookham Rise
COOKHAM
STATION HILL
STATION RD
ROMAN LEA
ELIZ CL
WESTWOOD GRN
MAIDENHEAD ROAD
LIGHTLANDS LA
STRAND LANE
White Brook
GRANGE LA
TERRYS LANE
GRANGE ROAD
BURNT OAK
PEARCE DRI
WAKELINS END
Grange Farm
LOWER ROAD
COXBORROW CL
SHERGOLD WAY
PEACE LA
School
Recreation Ground
Liby
WORSTER RD
NEW RD
GRAHAM RD
ROSE BANK CL
HALLDORE RD
LAUTREE GDNS
BRIAR GLEN
GORSE RD
BROOM HILL
SPENCERS LA
Gasholder
WINDMILL RD
HILLCREST AV
LYNDHURST AV
BRIDGE AV
SOUTHWOOD RD
CANNONDOWN RD
SOUTHWOOD GDNS
Strande Park Caravan Park
BASS MEAD
WHYTELADYES LA
THE SHAW
LESTERS RD
Lower Mount Farm
LONG LANE
Hillgrove Farm
BRADCUTTS LANE
Hillgrove Wood
ALLEYNS LANE
HILLS LANE
WARNERS HILL
Hardings Farm
Lea Farm
POPES LANE
KENNEL LANE
Hall
HARDINGS GRN
WESSONS HILL
Playing Field
COOKHAM DEAN BOTTOM
Cookham Dean
Woodlands Farm
SPRING LANE
STARTINS LANE
JOBS LA
DEAN LANE
WINTER HILL
KINGS LANE
King's Coppice Farm
SCHOOL LA
CHURCH LANE
Pigeonhouse Wood
REDWINS LA
HOLLYBUSH LA
STUBBLES LA
NWOOD CL
Bigfrith Common
HOCKETT LA
BIGFRITH LANE
COOMBE END
Cookhamdean Common
GRUBWOOD LANE
QUARRY WOOD ROAD
River Thames
RIVERWOOD AV
RIVERWOOD DRI

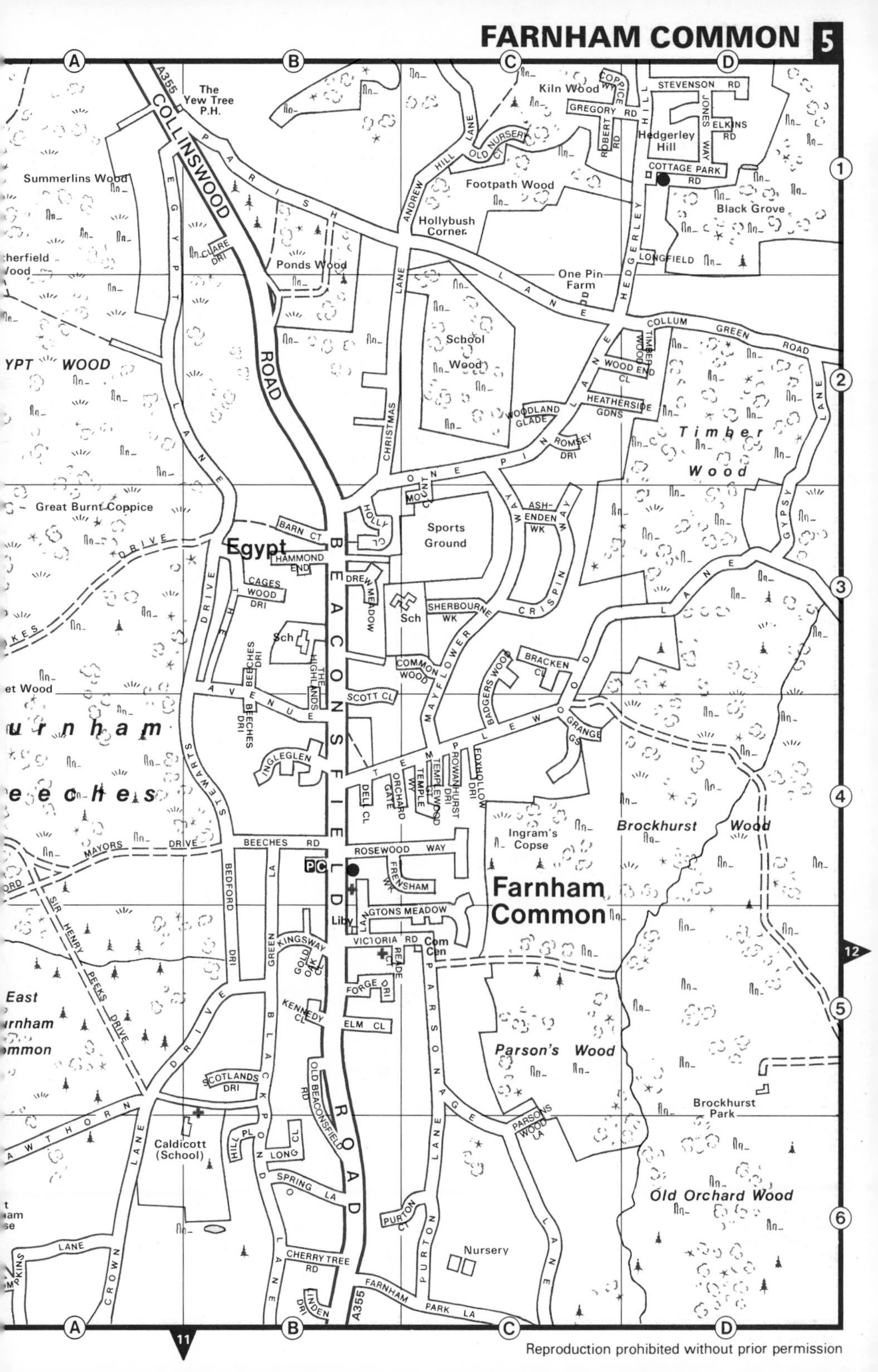
A
B
C
D
1
2
3
4
5
6
12
11
A355
COLLINSWOOD ROAD
The Yew Tree P.H.
PARISH LANE
Summerlins Wood
EGYPT LANE
CLARE DRI
Ponds Wood
Kiln Wood
COPPICE WAY
GREGORY RD
ROBERT RD
STEVENSON RD
JONES WAY
ELKINS RD
Hedgerley Hill
COTTAGE PARK RD
ANDREW HILL LANE
OLD NURSERY CT
Footpath Wood
Hollybush Corner
Black Grove
HEDGERLEY LANE
LONGFIELD
One Pin Farm
COLLUM GREEN ROAD
TIMBER WOOD
WOOD END CL
HEATHERSIDE GDNS
WOODLAND GLADE
ROMSEY DRI
School Wood
CHRISTMAS LANE
ONE PIN LANE
Timber Wood
GYPSY LANE
EGYPT WOOD
Great Burnt Coppice
BARN CT
HOLLY CL
MOUNT CL
Sports Ground
ASH-ENDEN WK
CRISPIN WAY
Egypt
HAMMOND END
CAGES WOOD DRI
DREW MEADOW
Sch
SHERBOURNE WK
THE DRIVE
Sch
BEECHES DRI
THE HIGHLANDS
COMMON WOOD
MAYFLOWER WAY
BRACKEN CL
BADGERS WOOD
AVENUE
SCOTT CL
LEWOOD
GRANGE GS
Burnham
Beeches
BEACONSFIELD ROAD
INGLEGLEN
TEMPLE WY
TEMPLEWOOD CL
ROWANHURST DRI
FOXHOLLOW DRI
DELL CL
ORCHARD GATE
Ingram's Copse
Brockhurst Wood
MAYORS DRIVE
BEECHES RD
ROSEWOOD WAY
FRENSHAM WK
STEWARTS DRIVE
BEDFORD DRI
GREEN LA
PC
Farnham Common
LANGTONS MEADOW
Liby
SIR HENRY PEEKS DRIVE
KINGSWAY
GOLD OAK CL
VICTORIA RD
READE CT
Com Cen
FORGE DRI
East Burnham Common
KENNEDY CL
ELM CL
Parson's Wood
PARSONAGE LANE
SCOTLANDS DRI
OLD BEACONSFIELD RD
BLACKPOND LANE
HAWTHORN LANE
Caldicott (School)
HILL PL
LONG CL
PARSONS WOOD LA
Brockhurst Park
SPRING LA
Old Orchard Wood
PURTON CT
PURTON LANE
CROWN LANE
Nursery
CHERRY TREE RD
LINDEN DRI
FARNHAM PARK LA

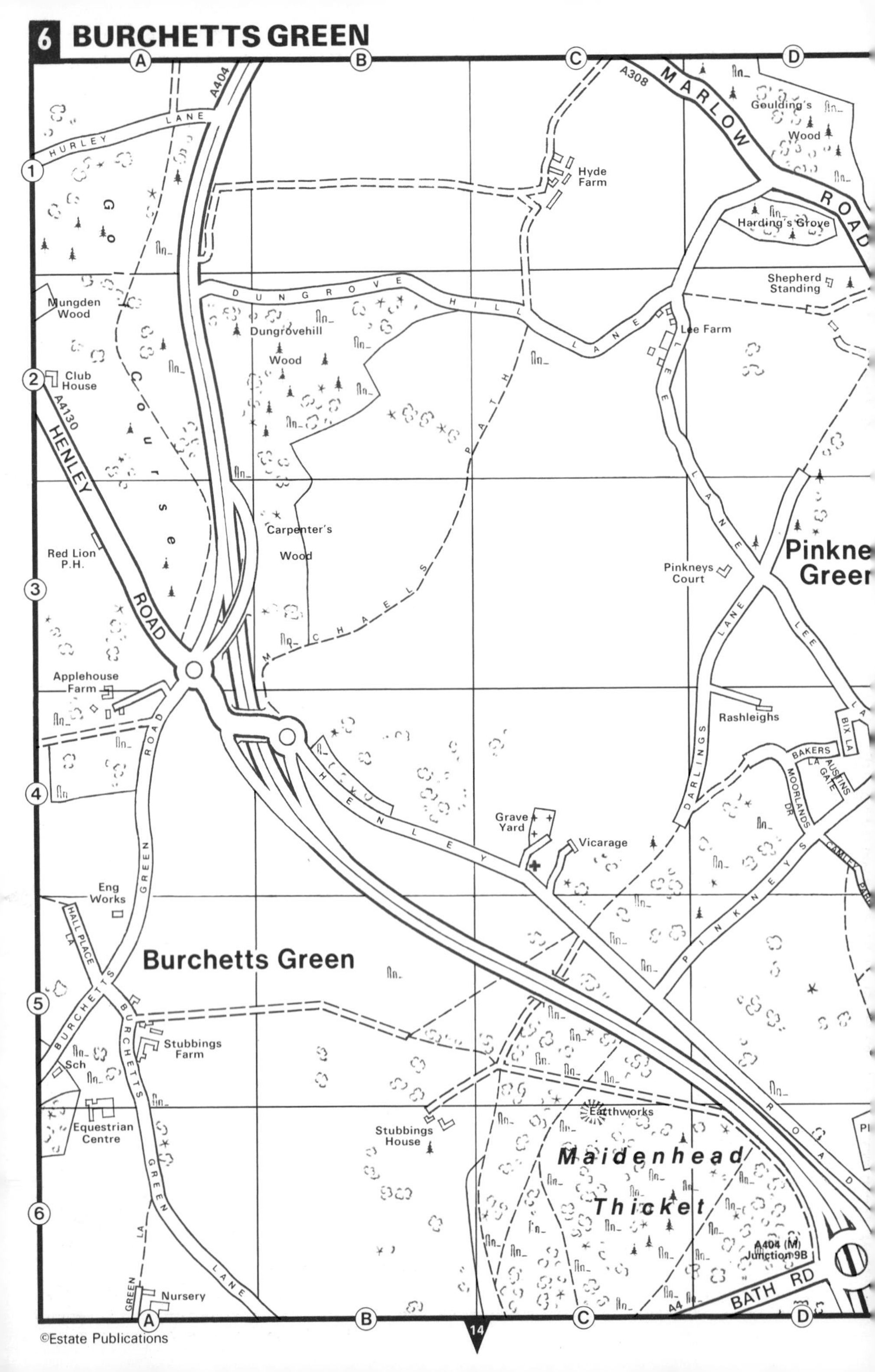
A
B
C
D
1
2
3
4
5
6
A404
A308
MARLOW ROAD
HURLEY LANE
Hyde Farm
Goulding's Wood
Harding's Grove
Shepherd Standing
Mungden Wood
DUNGROVE HILL LANE
Dungrovehill Wood
Lee Farm
LEE LANE
Club House
A4130
HENLEY ROAD
Golf Course
MICHAELS PATH
Carpenter's Wood
Pinkneys Green
Pinkneys Court
Red Lion P.H.
LEE LANE
DARLINGS LANE
Applehouse Farm
Rashleighs
BIX LA
BAKERS LA
AUSTINS GATE
MOORLANDS DR
GREEN ROAD
HENLEY ROAD
Grave Yard
Vicarage
CAMLEY PARK
PINKNEYS ROAD
Eng Works
HALL PLACE LA
Burchetts Green
BURCHETTS GREEN
Stubbings Farm
Sch
Equestrian Centre
Stubbings House
Earthworks
Maidenhead Thicket
A404 (M) Junction 9B
BATH RD
A4
GREEN LA
Nursery
LANE

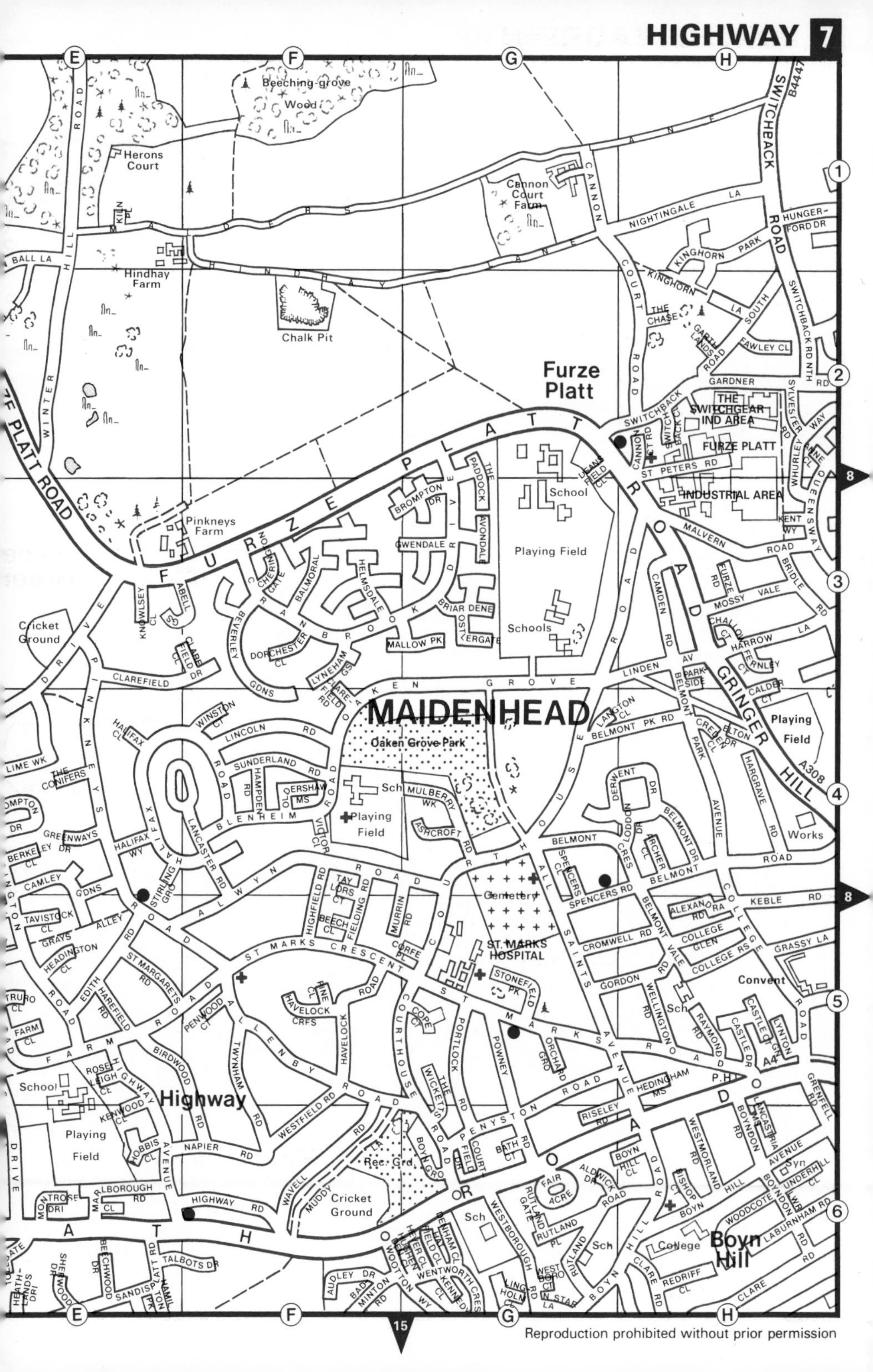

E
F
G
H
Beeching-grove Wood
Herons Court
Cannon Court Farm
Hindhay Farm
Chalk Pit
Furze Platt
Pinkneys Farm
Cricket Ground
THE SWITCHGEAR IND AREA
FURZE PLATT INDUSTRIAL AREA
School
Playing Field
Schools
MAIDENHEAD
Oaken Grove Park
Cemetery
ST. MARKS HOSPITAL
Convent
Works
Highway
Rec. Grd.
Cricket Ground
College
Boyn Hill
FURZE PLATT ROAD
WINTER HILL ROAD
BALL LA
CANNON LANE
NIGHTINGALE LA
HUNGERFORD DR
SWITCHBACK ROAD
B4447
KINGHORN PARK
KINGHORN LA
SOUTH FAWLEY CL
GARTHLANDS ROAD
GARDNER RD
SYLVESTER RD
SWITCHBACK RD NTH
WHURLEY WAY
QUEENSWAY
KENT WY
MALVERN ROAD
COURT ROAD
ST PETERS RD
CANNON CT RD
SWITCHBACK CL
DEANSFIELD CL
FURZE RD
MOSSY VALE
BRIDLE RD
CAMDEN RD
CHALLOW CT
HARROW LA
FERNLEY CT
CALDER CT
GRINGER HILL
A308
PINKNEYS DRIVE
CLAREFIELD DR
KNOWLSEY CL
ABELL GS
CHERINGTON GATE
CRANBROOK DRIVE
BALMORAL
HELMSDALE
BRIAR DENE
MALLOW PK
OSTERGATE
BROMPTON DR
GWENDALE
THE PADDOCK
AVONDALE
BEVERLEY GDNS
DORCHESTER CL
LYNEHAM GS
CLAREFIELD
OAKEN GROVE
LINDEN AV
PARKSIDE
BELMONT PARK AVENUE
CREDEN CL
ELTON
HARGRAVE RD
LANGTON CL
BELMONT PK RD
HOUSE
DERWENT DR
LODDON DR
ARCHER CL
BELMONT DR
BELMONT ROAD
KEBLE RD
ALEXANDRA RD
COLLEGE GLEN
COLLEGE RS
GRASSY LA
COLLEGE ROAD
CROMWELL RD
GORDON RD
BELMONT VALE
SPENCERS RD
SPENCERS CL
ALL SAINTS AVENUE
WELLINGTON RD
RAYMOND RD
CASTLE CT
CASTLE DR
LYNTON GN
A4
GRENFELL RD
HALIFAX CL
WINSTON CT
LINCOLN RD
SUNDERLAND RD
HAMPDEN RD
OLDERSHAW MS
VICTOR CL
VICTOR RD
MULBERRY WK
ASHCROFT RD
BLENHEIM RD
HALIFAX RD
HALIFAX WY
LANCASTER RD
STIRLING GRO
ALWYN ROAD
NORTH
HIGHFIELD RD
TAYLORS CT
FIELDING RD
MURRIN RD
BEECH CL
CORFE PL
ST MARKS CRESCENT
ST MARKS ROAD
STONEFIELD PK
LIME WK
THE CONIFERS
BROMPTON DR
GREENWAYS DR
BERKELEY CL
CAMLEY GDNS
TAVISTOCK CL
GRAYS ALLEY
HEADINGTON CL
EDITH RD
HAREFIELD RD
ST MARGARETS RD
PENWOOD CT
ALLENBY ROAD
BIRDWOOD RD
TWYNHAM RD
HAVELOCK CRES
HAVELOCK RD
PINE CL
COURTHOUSE RD
COPE CT
PORTLOCK RD
POWNEY RD
ORCHARD GRO
THE WICKETS
TRURO CL
FARM CL
FARM ROAD
ROSELEIGH CL
HIGHWAY
KENWOOD CL
HOBBIS DR
HIGHWAY AVENUE
WESTFIELD RD
NAPIER RD
HIGHWAY RD
WAVELL
MUDDY LA
BOYN GRO
FIELD CT
BATH CT
PENYSTON ROAD
HEDINGHAM MS
RISELEY RD
BOYN HILL CL
BOYN HILL ROAD
FAIR ACRE
ALDWICK DR
ALDWICK ROAD
RUTLAND GATE
RUTLAND PL
RUTLAND RD
WESTBOROUGH RD
WEST BORO CT
LINGHOLM CL
NORTH STAR LA
WESTMORLAND RD
BOYNDON RD
LANCASTRIA MS
AVENUE
SYN
UNDERHILL CL
BISHOP CT
BOYN
WOODCOTE
LAWRENCE RD
LABURNHAM RD
CLARE RD
REDRIFF CL
P.H.
BATH ROAD
MONTROSE DR
MARLBOROUGH RD
BROOK CL
SHERWOOD DR
BEECHWOOD DR
PLATT RD
TALBOTS DR
SANDISP PK
HAMIL
HEATHLANDS DR
AUDLEY DR
BADMINTON RD
WOOTTON WY
HEYNES FIELD
HUNTERS CL
DENHAM CL
WENTWORTH CRES
KENNEDY CL
DRIVE
1
2
3
4
5
6
8
15

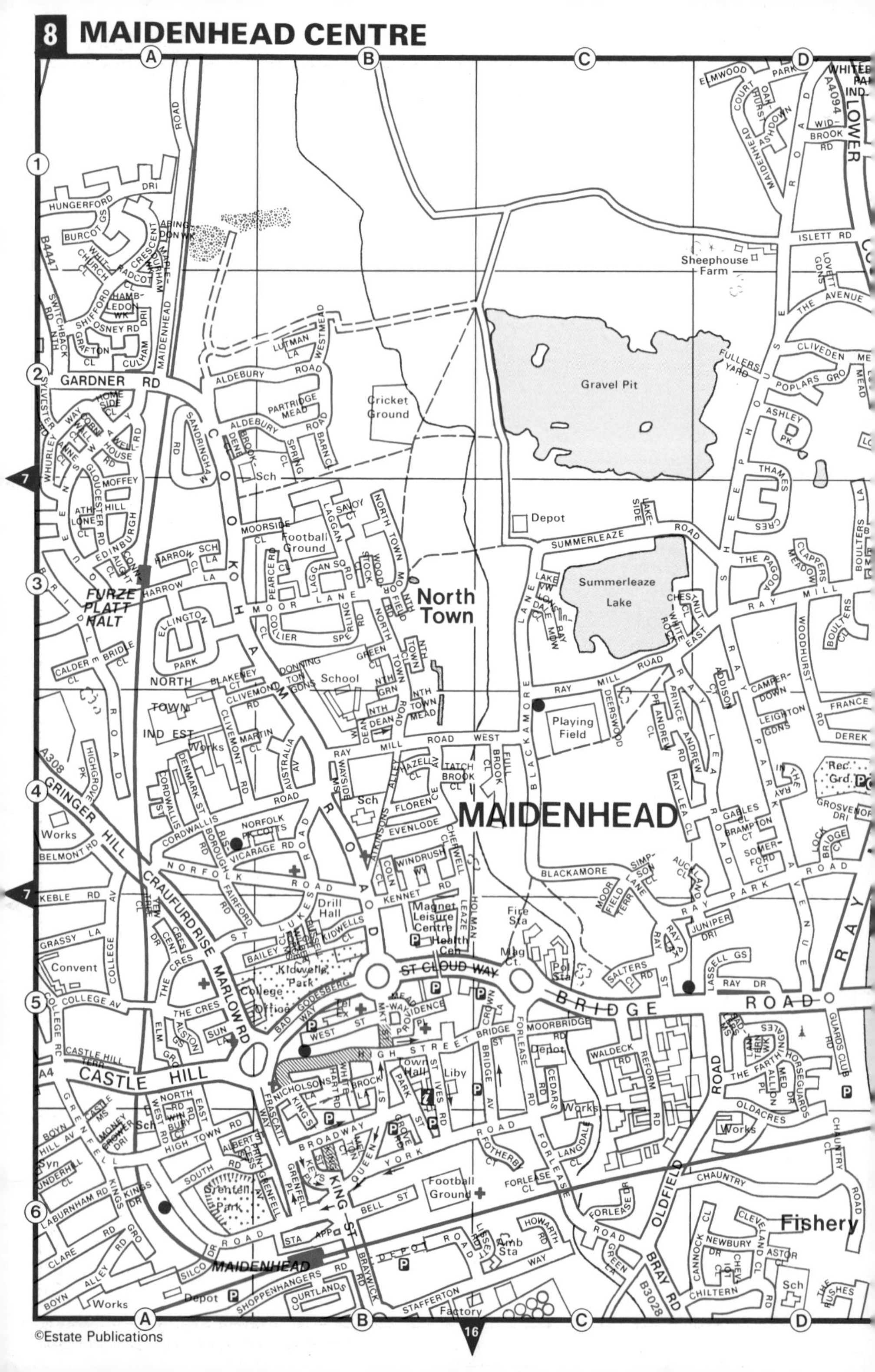
8
MAIDENHEAD CENTRE
MAIDENHEAD
North Town
Gravel Pit
Summerleaze Lake
Cricket Ground
Football Ground
Playing Field
Sheephouse Farm
FURZE PLATT HALT
NORTH TOWN IND EST
Kidwells Park
Grenfell Park
Magnet Leisure Centre
Fishery
GARDNER RD
CASTLE HILL
BRIDGE ROAD
ST CLOUD WAY
HIGH STREET
KING ST
RAY MILL ROAD WEST
RAY MILL ROAD EAST
SUMMERLEAZE ROAD
BLACKAMORE LANE
RAY PARK AVENUE
MARLOW RD
CRAUFURD RISE
GRINGER HILL
COOKHAM ROAD
OLDFIELD ROAD
BRAY RD
ISLETT RD
MAIDENHEAD
©Estate Publications
16

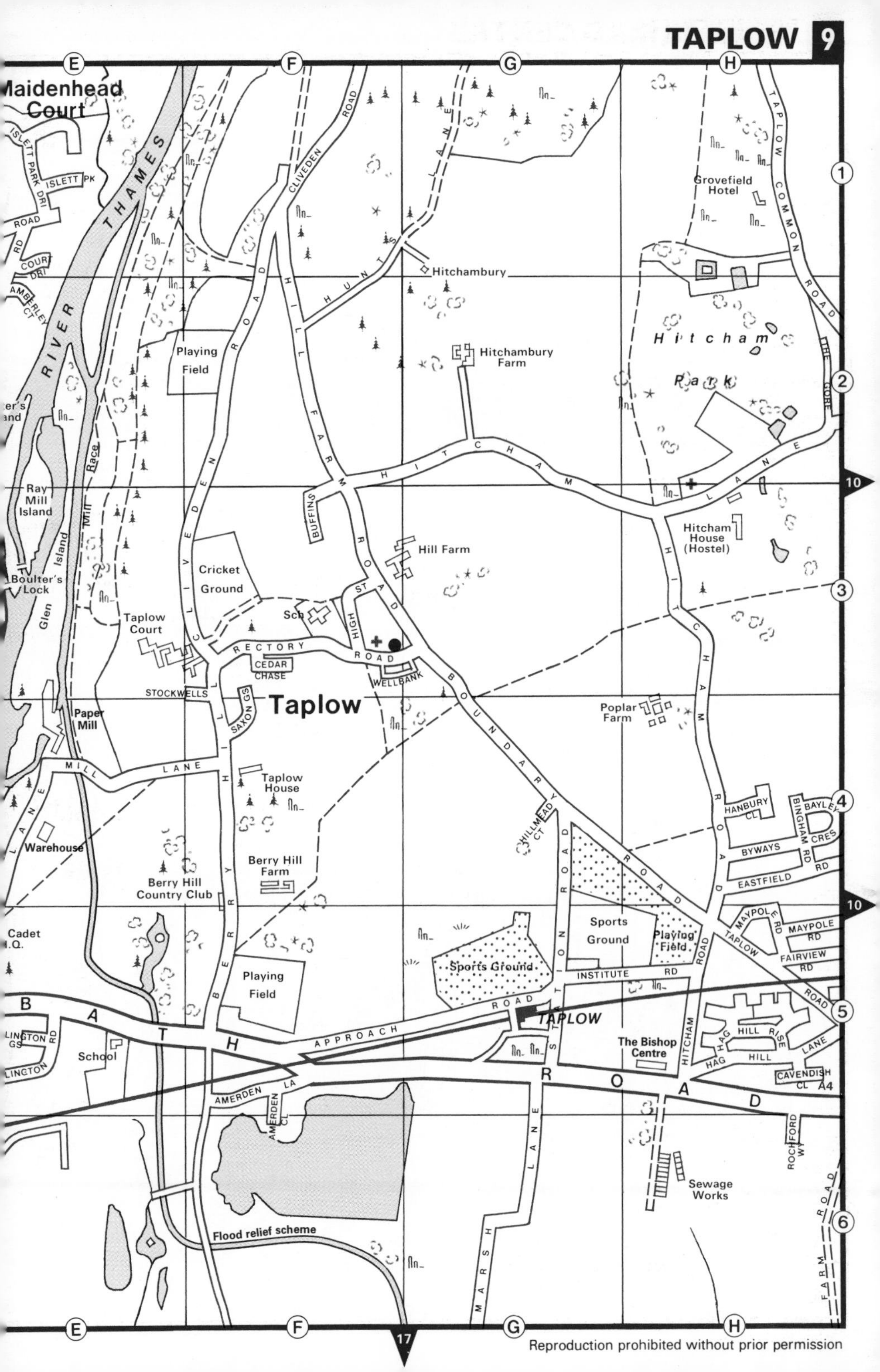
Maidenhead Court
RIVER THAMES
Playing Field
CLIVEDEN ROAD
HILL FARM ROAD
HUNTS LANE
Hitchambury
Hitchambury Farm
Grovefield Hotel
TAPLOW COMMON ROAD
Hitcham Park
THE GORE
HITCHAM LANE
BUFFINS
Hill Farm
Hitcham House (Hostel)
Ray Mill Island
Mill Race
Glen Island
Boulter's Lock
Cricket Ground
Taplow Court
Sch
HIGH ST
RECTORY ROAD
CEDAR CHASE
WELLBANK
STOCKWELLS
SAXON GS
Taplow
BOUNDARY ROAD
Poplar Farm
HITCHAM ROAD
Paper Mill
MILL LANE
Taplow House
HILLMEAD CT
HANBURY CL
BINGHAM RD
BAYLEY CRES
BYWAYS
EASTFIELD RD
Warehouse
Berry Hill Farm
Berry Hill Country Club
BERRY HILL
STATION ROAD
Sports Ground
Playing Field
MAYPOLE RD
MAYPOLE RD
FAIRVIEW RD
TAPLOW ROAD
Cadet H.Q.
Playing Field
Sports Ground
INSTITUTE RD
APPROACH ROAD
TAPLOW
BATH ROAD
School
The Bishop Centre
HAG HILL RISE
HAG HILL LANE
CAVENDISH CL
A4
AMERDEN LA
AMERDEN CL
MARSH LANE
ROCHFORD WY
Sewage Works
Flood relief scheme
FARM ROAD
E F G H
1 2 3 4 5 6
10
17

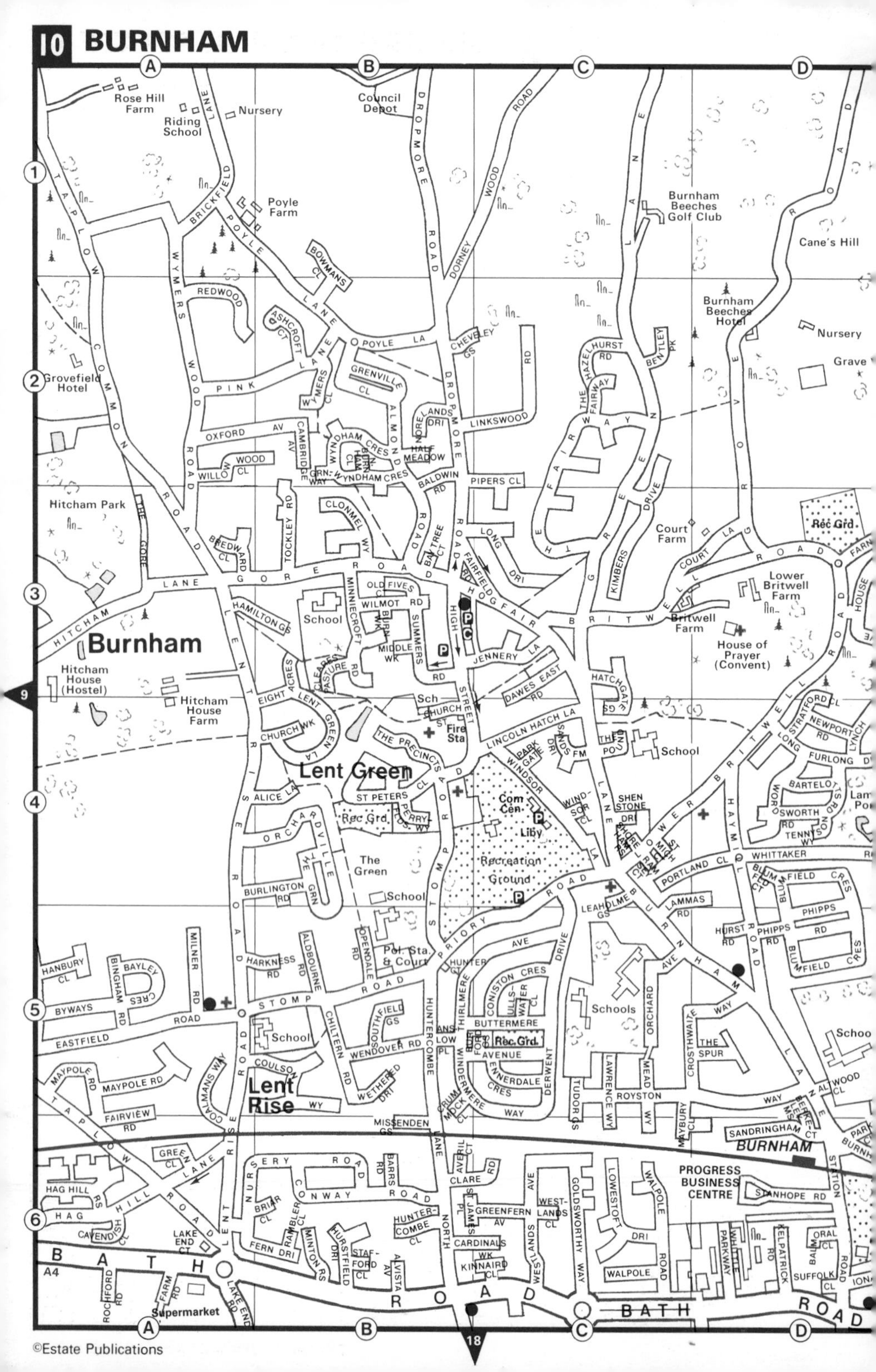

Rose Hill Farm
Riding School
Nursery
Council Depot
Poyle Farm
Burnham Beeches Golf Club
Cane's Hill
Burnham Beeches Hotel
Nursery
Grave
Grovefield Hotel
Hitcham Park
Court Farm
Rec Grd
Lower Britwell Farm
Britwell Farm
House of Prayer (Convent)
Burnham
Hitcham House (Hostel)
Hitcham House Farm
School
Sch
Fire Sta
Lent Green
Com Cen
Liby
Recreation Ground
The Green
School
Pol. Sta. & Court
Schools
Lent Rise
Rec Grd
BURNHAM
PROGRESS BUSINESS CENTRE
Supermarket
BATH ROAD
A4

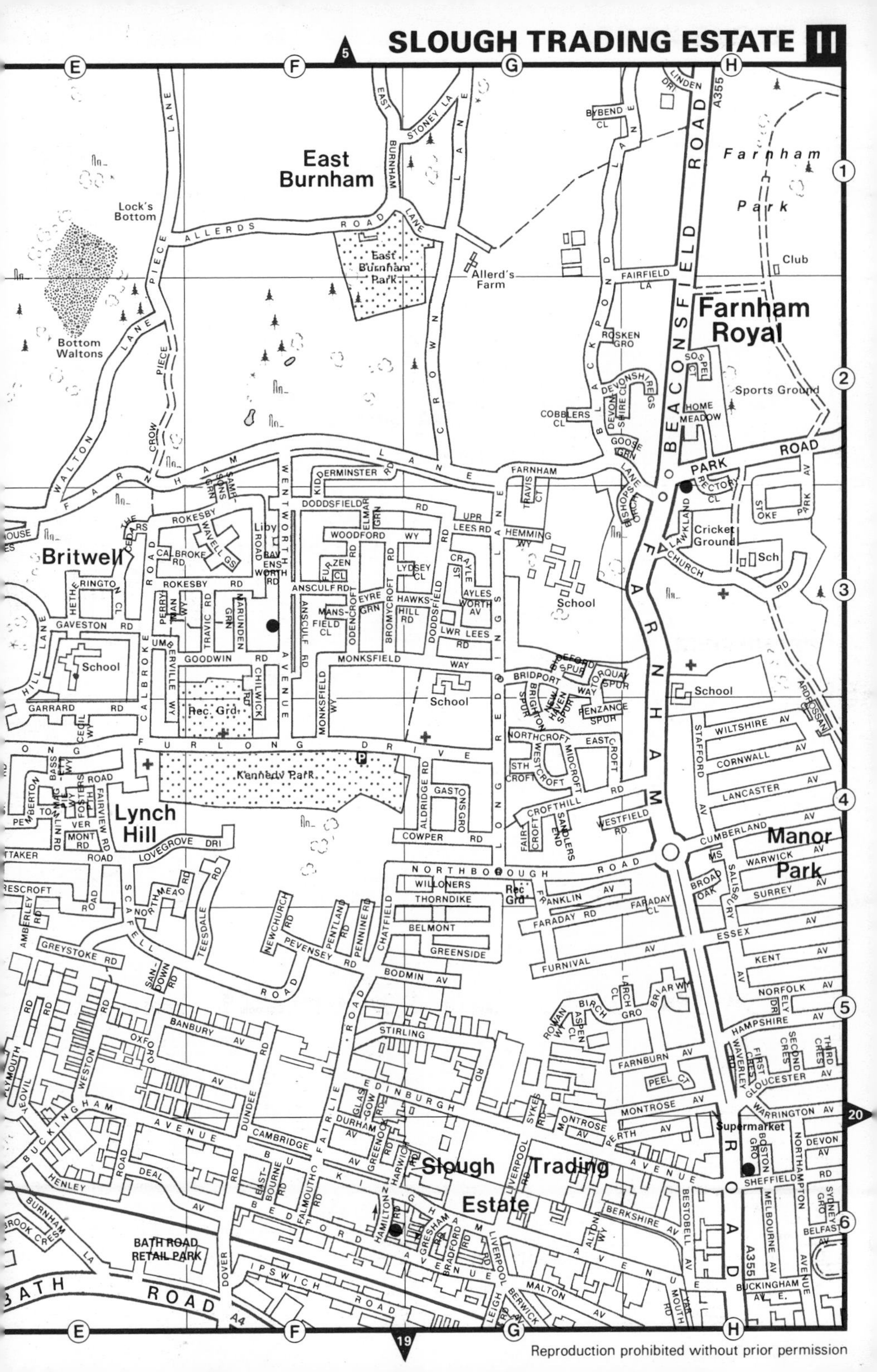
East Burnham
Lock's Bottom
Bottom Waltons
East Burnham Park
Allerd's Farm
Farnham Park
Club
Farnham Royal
Sports Ground
Britwell
School
Rec. Grd
Kennedy Park
Lynch Hill
Cricket Ground
Manor Park
Supermarket
Slough Trading Estate
BATH ROAD RETAIL PARK
BATH ROAD
FARNHAM ROAD
BEACONSFIELD ROAD
FARNHAM LANE
FARNHAM PARK ROAD
FURLONG DRIVE
NORTHBOROUGH ROAD
BUCKINGHAM AVENUE
EDINBURGH AV
BEDFORD AVENUE
IPSWICH ROAD
LIVERPOOL AV
CROWN LANE
ALLERDS ROAD
BURNHAM LANE
WALTON LANE
CROW PIECE LANE
LONG READINGS LANE
WENTWORTH AVENUE
A355
A4
E
F
G
H
1
2
3
4
5
6
5
19
20

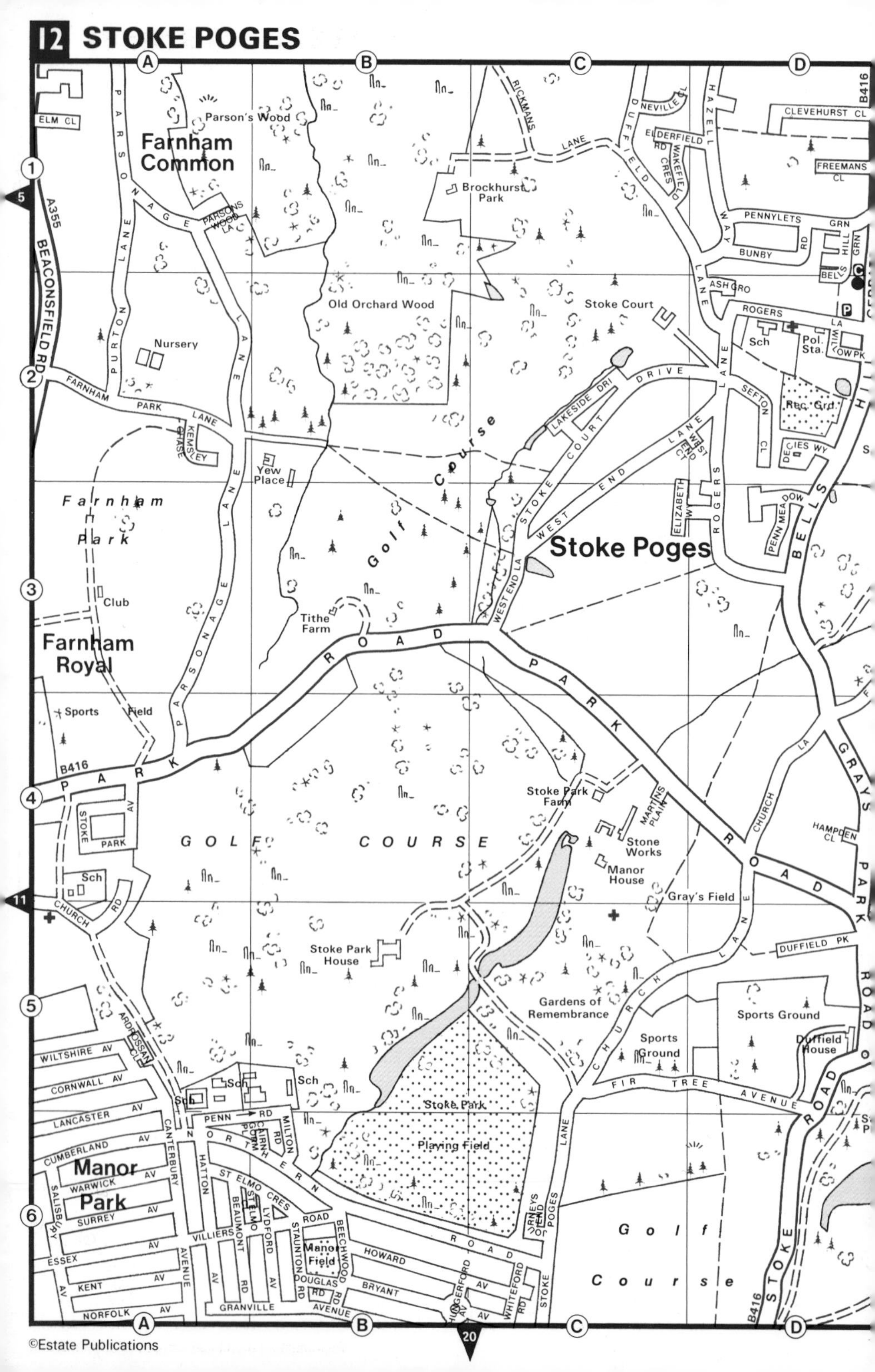
Farnham Common
Parson's Wood
Farnham Park
Farnham Royal
Manor Park
Stoke Poges
Brockhurst Park
Old Orchard Wood
Stoke Court
Nursery
Yew Place
Club
Tithe Farm
Golf Course
GOLF COURSE
Sports Field
Stoke Park Farm
Stone Works
Manor House
Gray's Field
Stoke Park House
Gardens of Remembrance
Sports Ground
Duffield House
Stoke Park Playing Field
Manor Field
Rec. Grd.
Pol. Sta.
Sch
BEACONSFIELD RD
A355
B416
PARSONAGE LANE
PURTON LANE
FARNHAM PARK LANE
PARSONS WOOD LA
KEMSLEY CHASE
ELM CL
PARK ROAD
STOKE PARK AV
CHURCH RD
ARDROSSAN CL
RICKMANS LANE
DUFFIELD LANE
NEVILLE CL
ELDERFIELD RD
WAKEFIELD CRES
HAZELL WAY
CLEVEHURST CL
FREEMANS CL
PENNYLETS GRN
BUNBY RD
HILL GRN
BELLS
ASH GRO
ROGERS LA
LAKESIDE DRI
STOKE COURT DRIVE
SEFTON CL
WEST END LANE
WEST END CT
WEST END LA
ELIZABETH WY
ROGERS
PENN MEADOW
BELLS HILL
DECIES WY
WILLOW PK
CHURCH LA
GRAYS PARK ROAD
HAMPDEN CL
MARTINS PLAIN
DUFFIELD PK
CHURCH LANE
FIR TREE AVENUE
STOKE ROAD
STOKE POGES LANE
JOURNEYS END
WILTSHIRE AV
CORNWALL AV
LANCASTER AV
CUMBERLAND AV
WARWICK AV
SURREY AV
SALISBURY AV
ESSEX AV
KENT AV
NORFOLK AV
CANTERBURY AVENUE
HATTON AV
PENN RD
CAIRNGORM PL
MILTON RD
NORTHERN ROAD
ST ELMO CRES
ST ELMO CL
BEAUMONT RD
LYDFORD AV
STAUNTON ROAD
BEECHWOOD RD
VILLIERS RD
HOWARD AV
BRYANT AV
DOUGLAS RD
GRANVILLE AVENUE
HUNGERFORD AV
WHITEFORD RD
A B C D
1 2 3 4 5 6
5 11 20

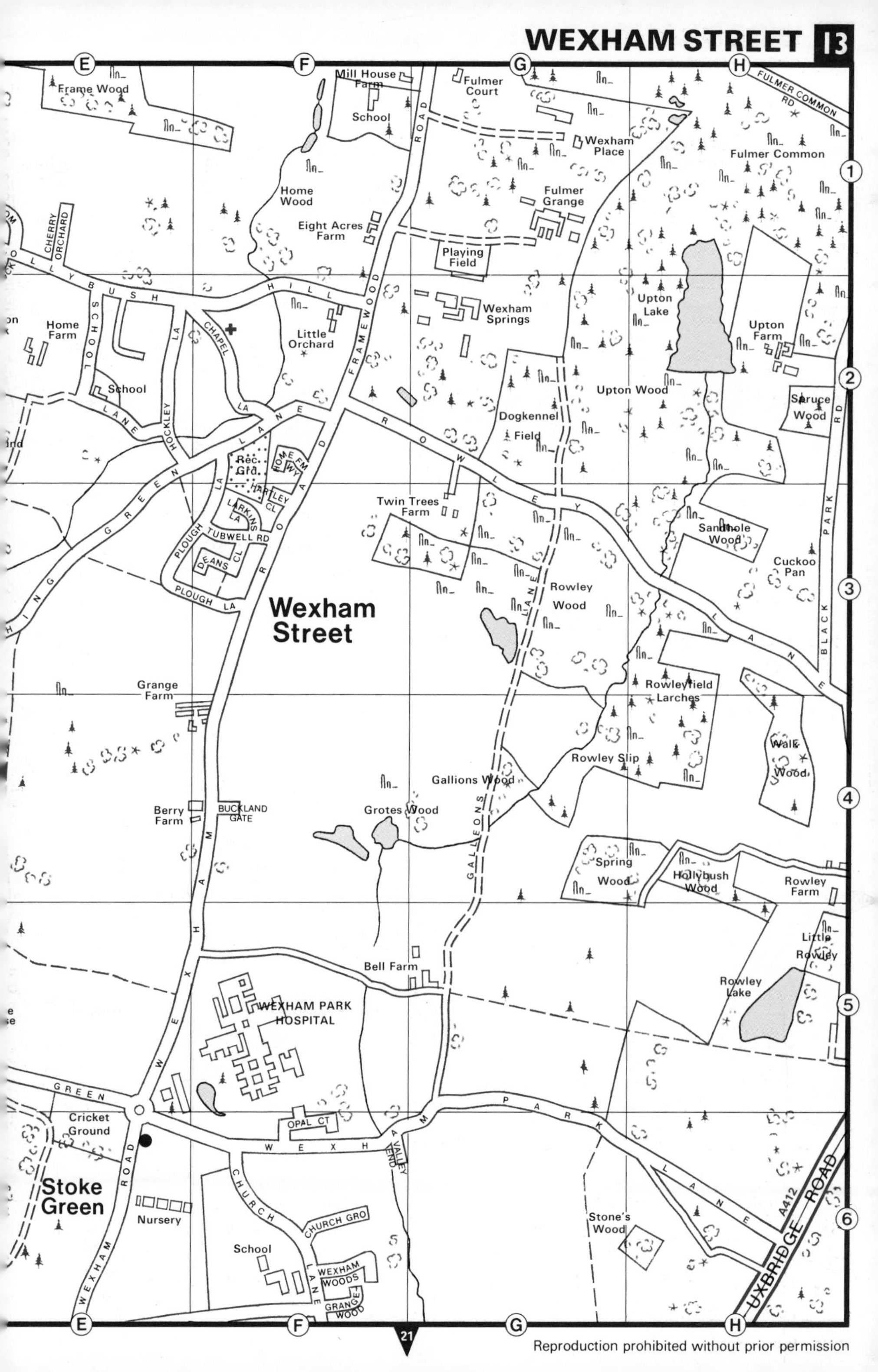

Reproduction prohibited without prior permission

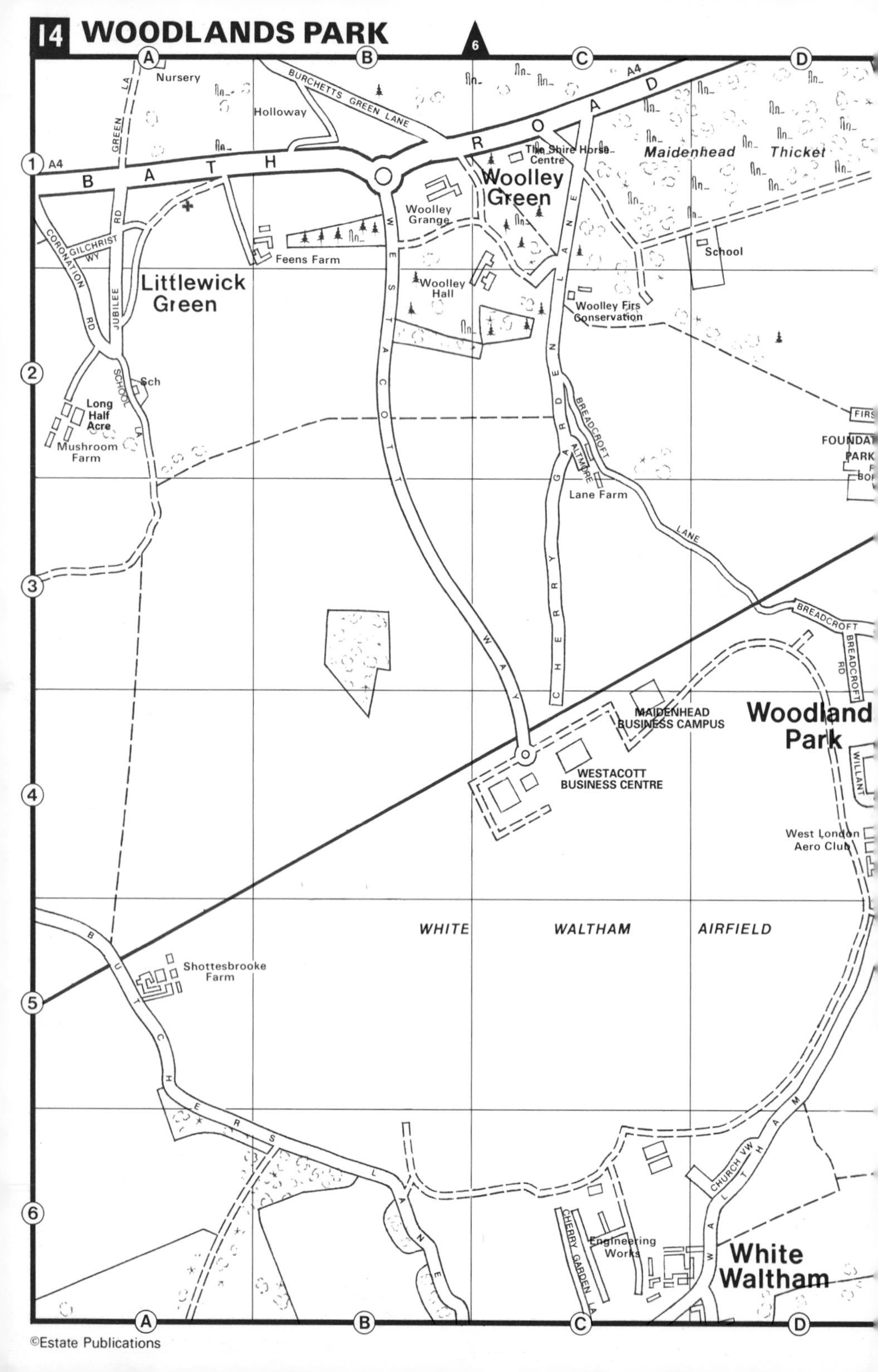

6

Maidenhead Thicket

Woolley Green

Woolley Grange

The Shire Horse Centre

Nursery

Holloway

BURCHETTS GREEN LANE

GREEN LA

BATH ROAD

A4

Feens Farm

Littlewick Green

Woolley Hall

Woolley Firs Conservation

School

Sch

Long Half Acre

Mushroom Farm

CORONATION RD

GILCHRIST WY

JUBILEE

SCHOOL LA

WESTACOTT WAY

CHERRY GARDEN LANE

BREADCROFT

ALTMORE

Lane Farm

LANE

BREADCROFT

BREADCROFT RD

FIRS

FOUNDAT PARK

MAIDENHEAD BUSINESS CAMPUS

Woodland Park

WESTACOTT BUSINESS CENTRE

West London Aero Club

WILLANT

WHITE   WALTHAM   AIRFIELD

Shottesbrooke Farm

CHERRY LANE

CHURCH VW

WALTHAM

Engineering Works

CHERRY GARDEN LA

White Waltham

A   B   C   D

1

2

3

4

5

6

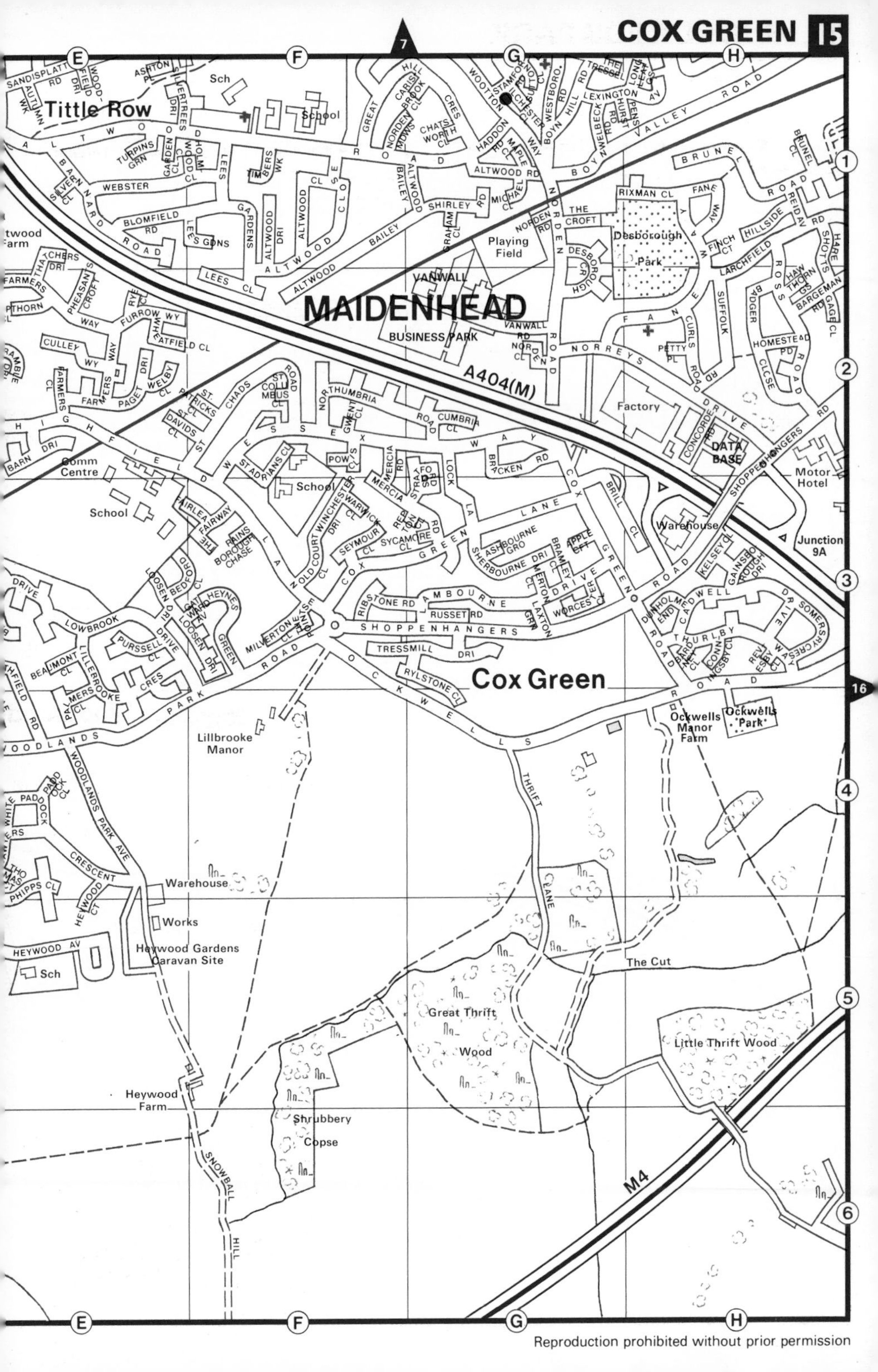
Tittle Row
MAIDENHEAD
Cox Green
A404(M)
M4
ALTWOOD ROAD
ALTWOOD BAILEY
ALTWOOD CLOSE
ALTWOOD DRI
ALTWOOD RD
ALTWOOD CL
BOYN VALLEY ROAD
BOYN HILL RD
NORDEN ROAD
NORDEN RD
NORDEN CL
BRUNEL ROAD
BRUNEL CL
RIXMAN CL
FANE WAY
NORREYS DRIVE
SHOPPENHANGERS ROAD
SHOPPENHANGERS RD
COX GREEN LANE
COX GREEN ROAD
WESSEX WAY
HIGHFIELD LANE
OCKWELLS ROAD
WOODLANDS PARK AVE
WOODLANDS PARK RD
BARN DRI
BRACKEN RD
LAMBOURNE DRIVE
SHERBOURNE DRI
TRESSMILL DRI
RYLSTONE CL
RIBSTONE RD
RUSSET RD
MILVERTON CL
LOOSEN DRIVE
LILLEBROOKE CRES
PARK ROAD
BEAUMONT CL
PALMERS CL
SNOWBALL HILL
THRIFT LANE
HEYWOOD AV
HEYWOOD CT
PHIPPS CL
CRESCENT
WHITE PADDOCK
WEBSTER CL
BLOMFIELD RD
BARNARD ROAD
LEES GARDENS
LEES GDNS
LEES CL
TIMBERS WK
TURPINS GRN
FARMERS WAY
FARMERS CL
PHEASANTS CROFT
CULLEY WY
PAGET DRI
WELBY CL
FURROW WY
WHEATFIELD CL
THATCHERS DRI
ST. CHADS ROAD
ST. PATRICKS CL
ST. DAVIDS CL
ST. COLUMBUS CL
NORTHUMBRIA
CUMBRIA CL
GWENT CL
MERCIA RD
STRATFORD
SEYMOUR CL
SYCAMORE CL
WARWICK CL
WINCHESTER DRI
OLD COURT CL
FAIRLEA
THE FAIRWAY
RAINSBOROUGH CHASE
BEDFORD CL
HEYNES GREEN
LOWBROOK DRIVE
PURSSELL CL
ASHBOURNE GRO
BRAMLEY CL
APPLE CFT
BRILL CL
MERTON CL
LAXTON GRN
WORCESTER CL
KELSEY CL
GAINSBOROUGH DRIVE
CADWELL DRIVE
THURLBY WAY
SOMERS CRES
DUNHOLME END
CONNINGSBY CL
DESBOROUGH CR
HILLSIDE
LARCHFIELD RD
FINCH CT
SUFFOLK
CURLS ROAD
PETTY PL
ROSS RD
HOMESTEAD ROAD
BADGER
BARGEMAN
CONCORDE RD
THE CROFT
SHIRLEY RD
GRAHAM CL
MICHAEL CL
MAPLE CL
HADDON RD
GREAT HILL CRES
CHATSWORTH CL
NORDEN MDWS
WESTBOROUGH RD
WELBECK RD
LEXINGTON AV
VANWALL RD
Desborough Park
Playing Field
VANWALL BUSINESS PARK
Factory
DATA BASE
Motor Hotel
Warehouse
Junction 9A
School
Sch
Comm Centre
Lillbrooke Manor
Ockwells Manor Farm
Ockwells Park
Works
Heywood Gardens Caravan Site
Heywood Farm
Great Thrift Wood
Little Thrift Wood
Shrubbery Copse
The Cut
E
F
G
H
1
2
3
4
5
6
7
16

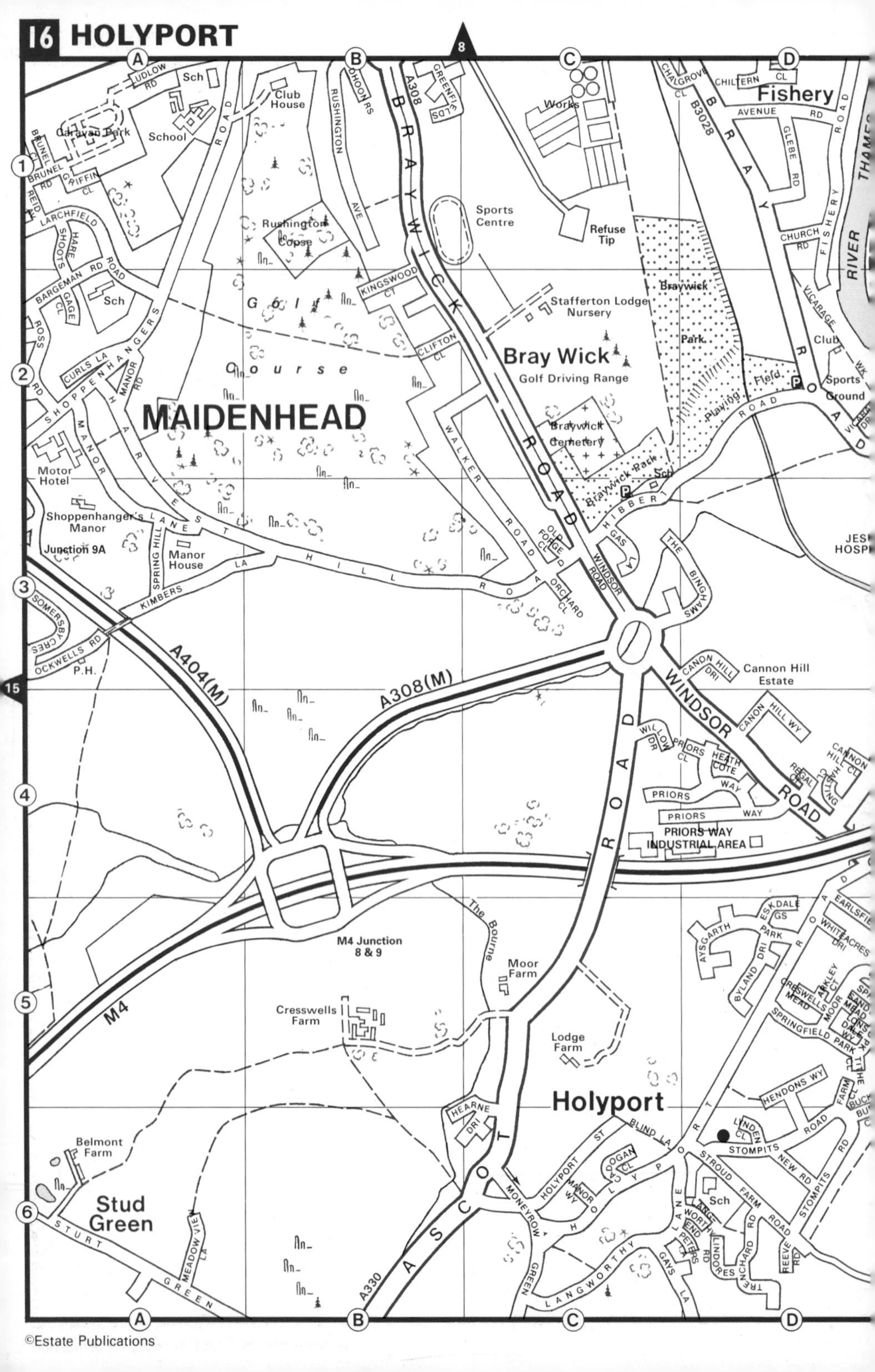
MAIDENHEAD
Bray Wick
Holyport
Fishery
Stud Green
Golf Course
Caravan Park
School
Sch
Club House
Rushington Copse
Sports Centre
Refuse Tip
Works
Stafferton Lodge Nursery
Golf Driving Range
Braywick Cemetery
Braywick Park
Playing Field
Club
Sports Ground
Motor Hotel
Shoppenhanger's Manor
Junction 9A
Manor House
P.H.
Cannon Hill Estate
PRIORS WAY INDUSTRIAL AREA
M4 Junction 8 & 9
Moor Farm
Cresswells Farm
Lodge Farm
Belmont Farm
The Bourne
RIVER THAMES
BRAYWICK ROAD
A308
A404(M)
A308(M)
M4
A330
B3028
WINDSOR ROAD
ASCOT ROAD
SHOPPENHANGERS ROAD
HARVEST HILL ROAD
WALKER ROAD
BRAY ROAD
STURT GREEN
LANGWORTHY LA
HOLYPORT ROAD
STROUD FARM ROAD
STOMPITS RD
©Estate Publications

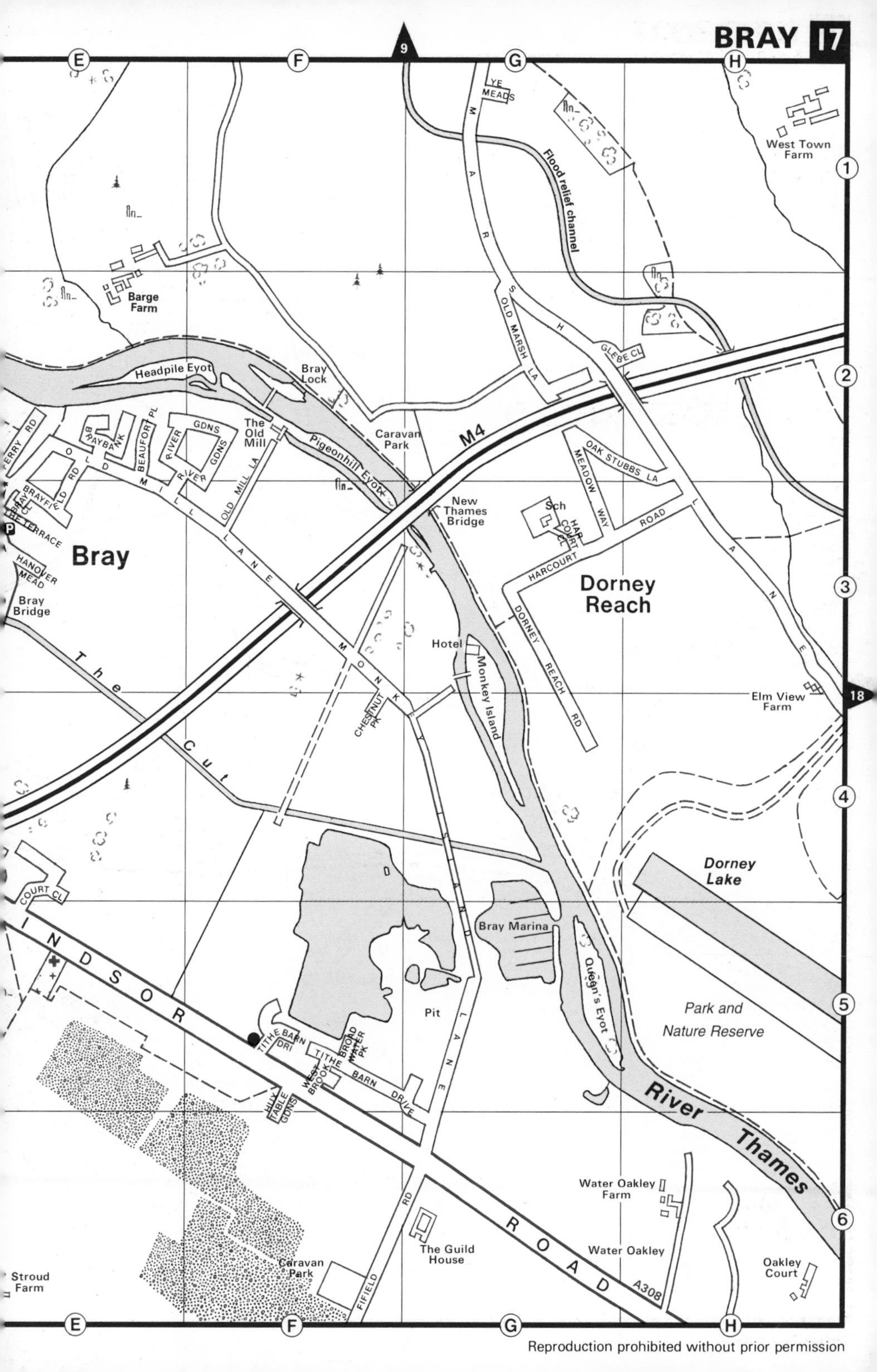

9

E F G H

West Town Farm

1

YE MEADS

Flood relief channel

M
A
R
S
H

OLD MARSH LA

Barge Farm

GLEBE CL

2

Headpile Eyot

Bray Lock

Caravan Park

M4

OAK STUBBS LA

FERRY RD

BRAYBANK

BEAUFORT PL

GDNS

RIVER GDNS

The Old Mill

Pigeonhill Eyot

OLD MILL LA

New Thames Bridge

Sch

HARCOURT CLOSE

MEADOW WAY

ROAD

BRAYFK

OLD

RD

TERRACE

HANOVER MEAD

Bray

HARCOURT

Dorney Reach

3

Bray Bridge

The

Cut

M
O
N
K
E
Y

CHESTNUT PK

Hotel

Monkey Island

DORNEY REACH RD

Elm View Farm

18

4

Dorney Lake

COURT CL

Bray Marina

Otego's Eyot

Park and Nature Reserve

5

W
I
N
D
S
O
R

Pit

TITHE BARN DRI

TITHE BARN DRIVE

BROAD WATER PK

BARN DRIVE

LANE

River Thames

6

Stroud Farm

Caravan Park

TABLE GDNS

WESSEX BROOK

FIFIELD RD

The Guild House

Water Oakley Farm

Water Oakley

A308

Oakley Court

R O A D

E F G H

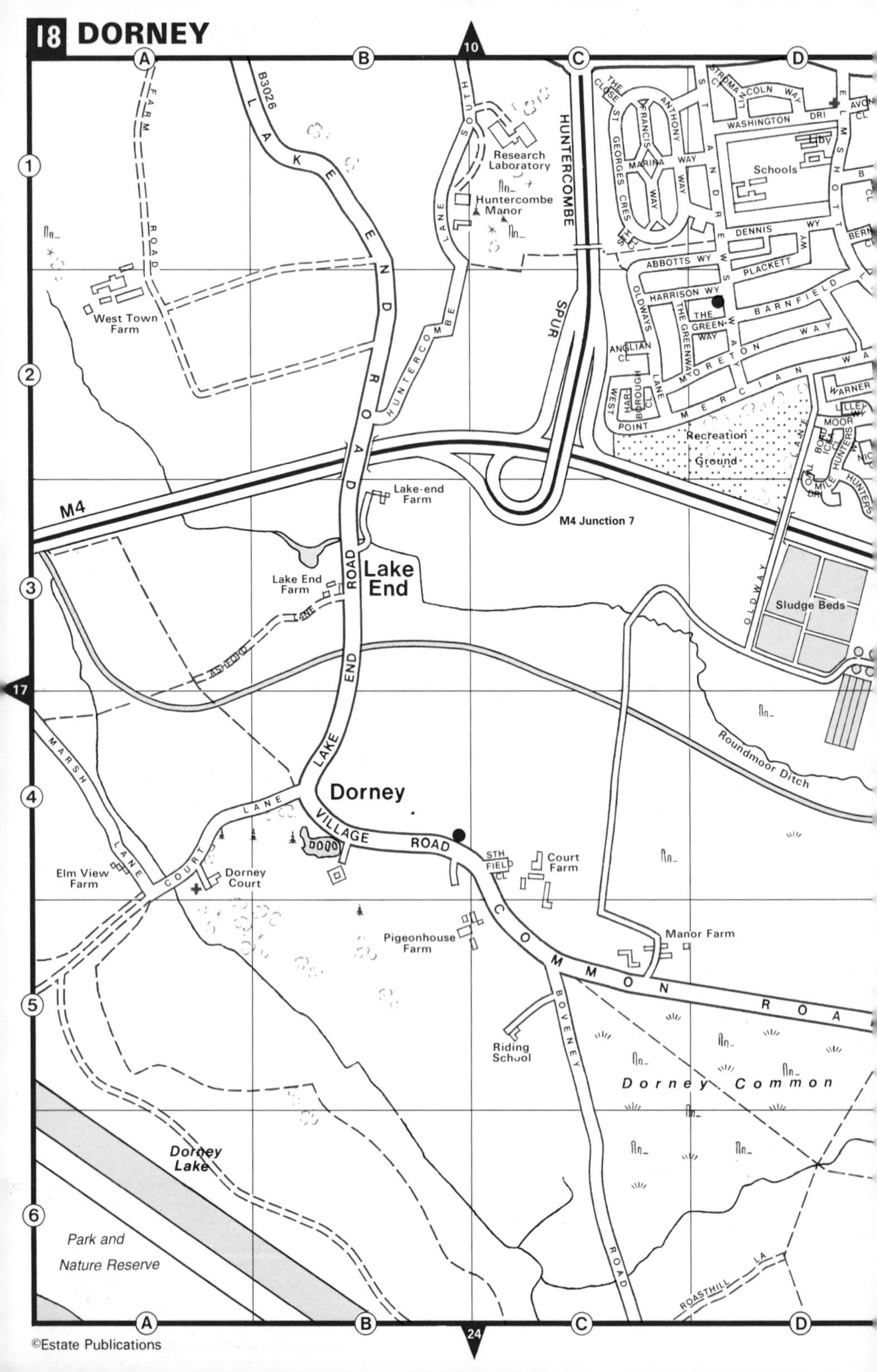

A
B
C
D
10
24
17
1
2
3
4
5
6
FARM ROAD
B3026
LAKE END ROAD
SOUTH LANE
Research Laboratory
Huntercombe Manor
HUNTERCOMBE SPUR
HUNTERCOMBE LANE
West Town Farm
THE CLOSE
ST GEORGES CRES
FRANCIS WAY
ANTHONY WAY
MARINA WAY
ST ANDREWS WAY
STROMA CT
LINCOLN WAY
WASHINGTON DRI
ELMSHOTT
AVON CL
Liby
Schools
DENNIS WY
ABBOTTS WY
PLACKETT WY
HARRISON WY
BARNFIELD
THE GREEN-WAY
THE GREENWAY
OLDWAYS
MORETON WAY
ANGLIAN CL
HARBOROUGH CL
WEST POINT
LANE
MERCIAN WAY
WARNER
Recreation Ground
M4
Lake-end Farm
M4 Junction 7
Lake End Farm
Lake End
ASHFORD LANE
OLDWAY
Sludge Beds
Roundmoor Ditch
MARSH LANE
Dorney
COURT LANE
VILLAGE ROAD
STH FIELD CL
Court Farm
Elm View Farm
Dorney Court
Pigeonhouse Farm
Manor Farm
COMMON ROAD
BOVENEY ROAD
Riding School
Dorney Common
Dorney Lake
Park and Nature Reserve
ROASTHILL LA

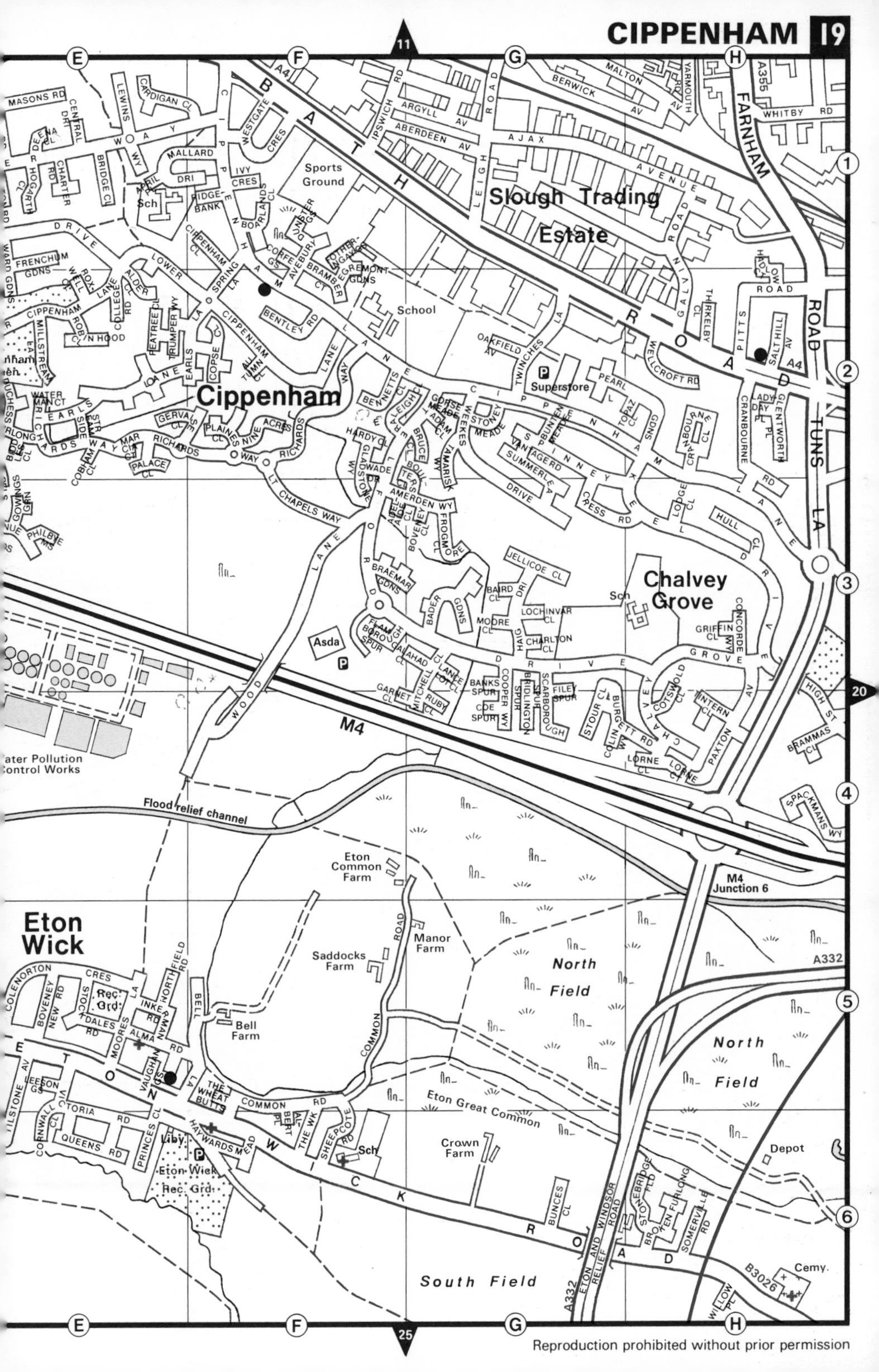
Cippenham
Slough Trading Estate
Chalvey Grove
Eton Wick
Sports Ground
School
Superstore
Asda
M4
M4 Junction 6
Flood relief channel
Water Pollution Control Works
Eton Common Farm
Manor Farm
Saddocks Farm
Bell Farm
North Field
Eton Great Common
Crown Farm
South Field
Depot
Cemy.
BATH ROAD
FARNHAM ROAD
TUNS LA
CIPPENHAM LANE
LOWER CIPPENHAM LA
WOOD LANE
ETON WICK ROAD
ETON AND WINDSOR RELIEF ROAD
COMMON ROAD
A4
A355
A332
B3026
11
20
25

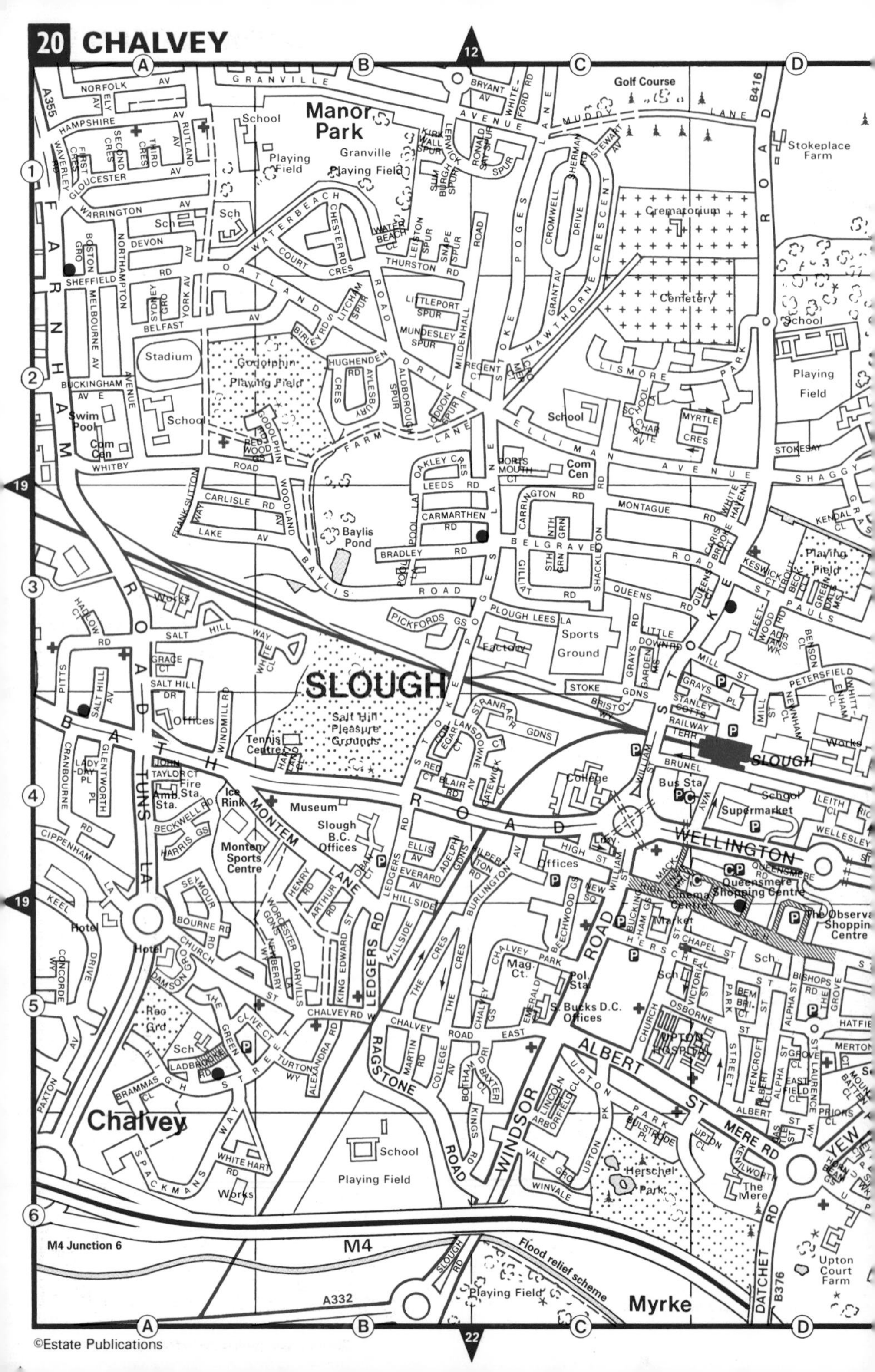

20 CHALVEY
12
19
22
A
B
C
D
1
2
3
4
5
6
Manor Park
Granville Playing Field
Playing Field
School
Golf Course
Stokeplace Farm
Crematorium
Cemetery
Stadium
Godolphin Playing Field
Swim Pool
Com Cen
Baylis Pond
SLOUGH
Salt Hill Pleasure Grounds
Tennis Centre
Sports Ground
Factory
Works
Offices
Fire Sta.
Amb. Sta.
Ice Rink
Museum
Slough B.C. Offices
Montem Sports Centre
Hotel
Rec Grd
Chalvey
College
Bus Sta
Supermarket
Queensmere Shopping Centre
The Observatory Shopping Centre
Cinema Centre
Market
Lby.
Mag. Ct.
Pol. Sta.
S. Bucks D.C. Offices
Upton Hospital
Herschel Park
The Mere
Upton Court Farm
Playing Field
Flood relief scheme
Myrke
M4 Junction 6
M4
A332
A355
A416
B416
B376
FARNHAM ROAD
GRANVILLE AV
NORFOLK AV
HAMPSHIRE AV
GLOUCESTER AV
WARRINGTON AV
DEVON AV
SHEFFIELD RD
BELFAST AV
BUCKINGHAM AVENUE
WHITBY ROAD
OATLAND DRIVE
WATERBEACH COURT
CHESTER RD
FARM LANE
STOKE POGES LANE
MUDDY LANE
STOKE ROAD
ELLIMAN AVENUE
SHAGGY CALF LANE
MONTAGUE RD
BELGRAVE ROAD
BAYLIS ROAD
QUEENS RD
MILL ST
PETERSFIELD AV
ST PAULS AV
SALT HILL WAY
BATH ROAD
TUNS LA
MONTEM LANE
WELLINGTON ST
HIGH ST
CHALVEY ROAD EAST
CHALVEY RD W
HIGH STREET
ALBERT ST
WINDSOR ROAD
RAGSTONE ROAD
UPTON PK
SPACKMANS WAY
WHITE HART RD
DATCHET RD
YEW TREE RD
SLOUGH RD
SLOUGH
©Estate Publications

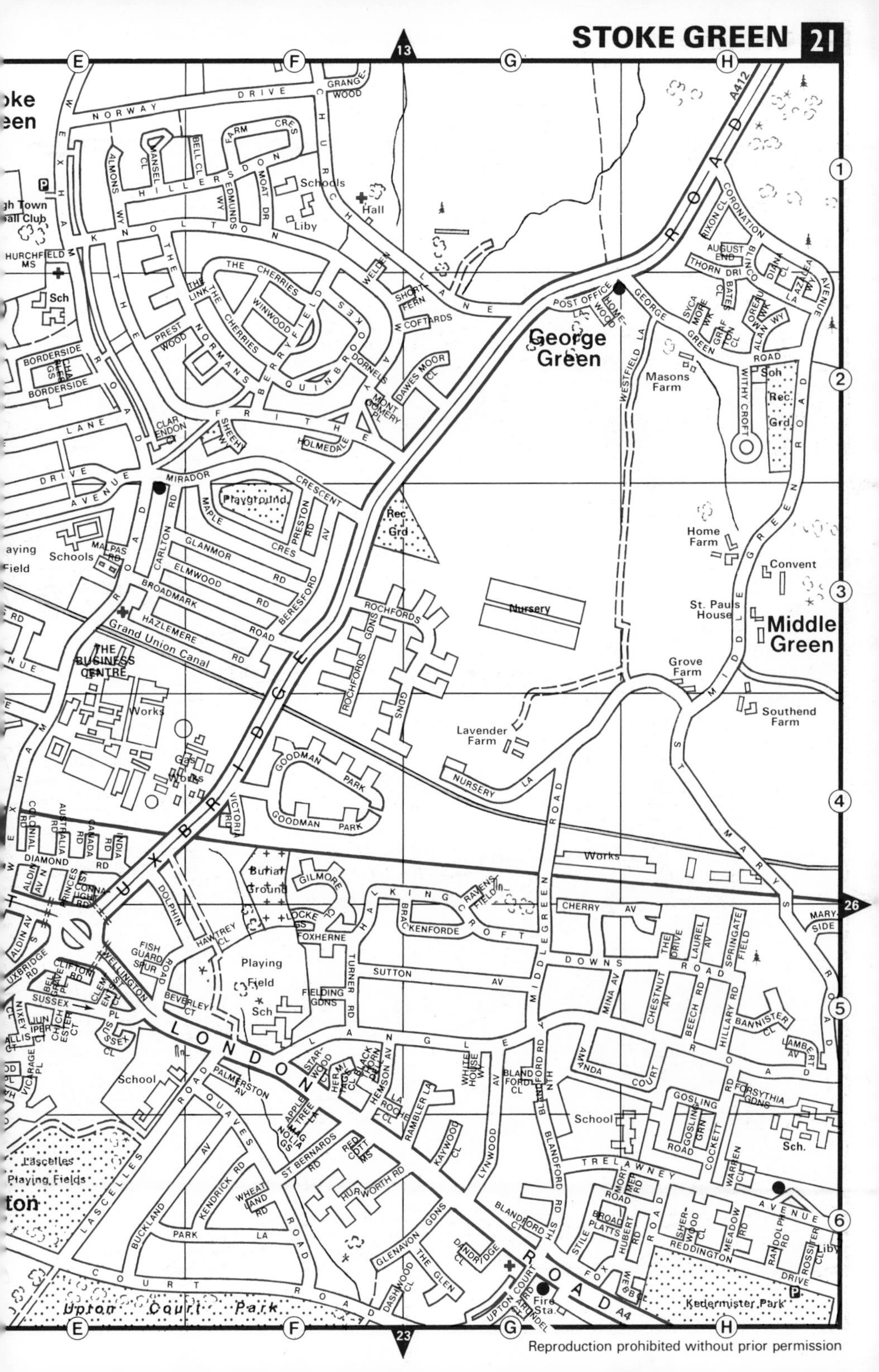
George Green
Middle Green
Masons Farm
Home Farm
Convent
St. Pauls House
Grove Farm
Southend Farm
Lavender Farm
Nursery
Grand Union Canal
THE BUSINESS CENTRE
Works
Gas Works
Burial Ground
Playing Field
Playground
Rec. Grd
Schools
Hall
Liby
Lascelles Playing Fields
Upton Court Park
Kedermister Park
Fire Sta.
UXBRIDGE ROAD
LONDON ROAD
A412
A4
NORWAY DRIVE
KNOLTON WAY
CHURCH LANE
WEXHAM ROAD
MIDDLEGREEN ROAD
ST MARYS ROAD
LANGLEY ROAD
HALKINGCROFT
DOWNS ROAD
TRELAWNEY AVENUE
REDDINGTON DRIVE
NURSERY LA
WESTFIELD LA
GOODMAN PARK
ROCHFORDS GDNS
MIRADOR CRESCENT
GEORGE GREEN ROAD
CORONATION AVENUE
COURT ROAD

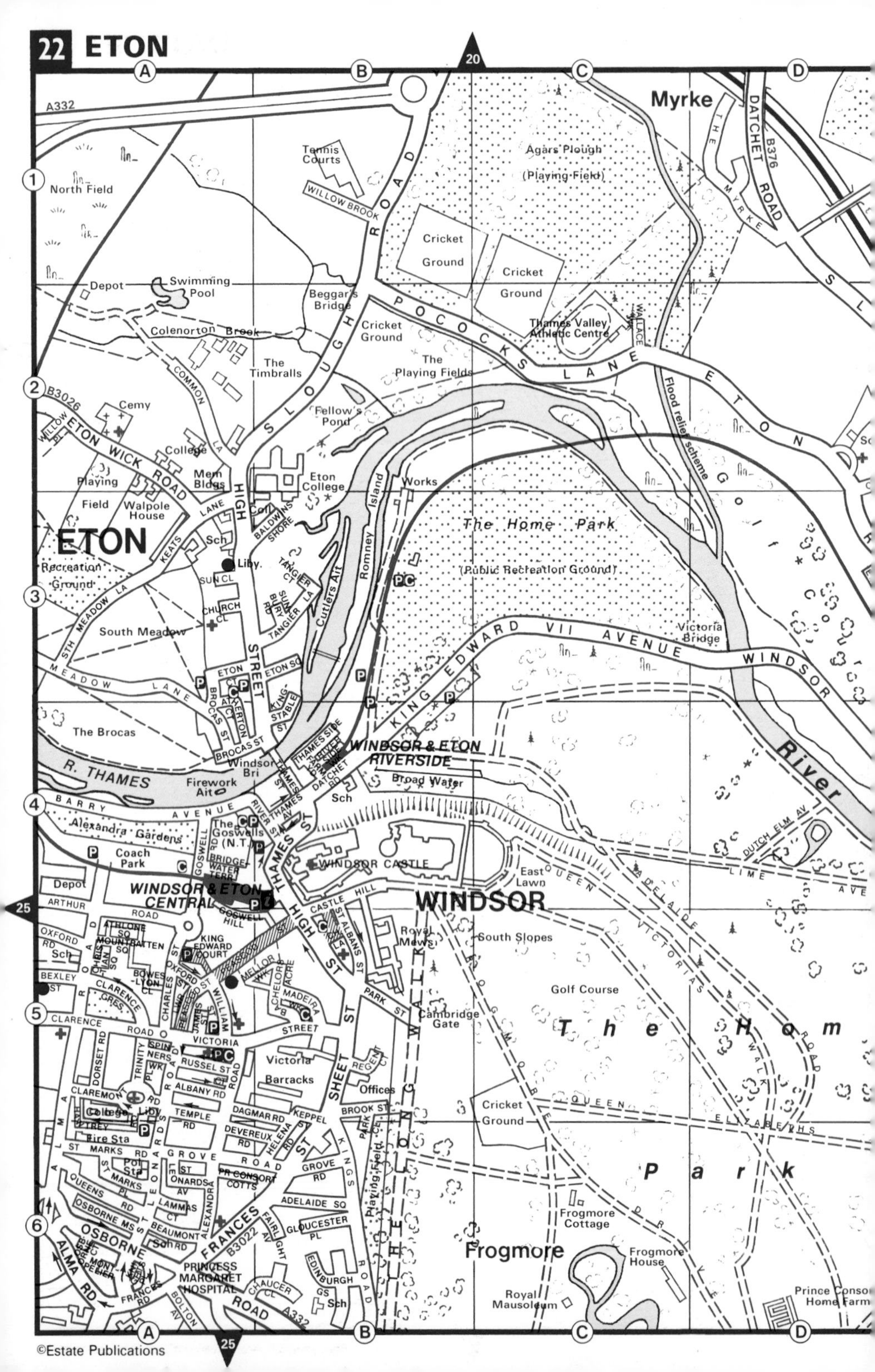

Myrke
Agars Plough
(Playing Field)
North Field
Tennis Courts
Cricket Ground
Swimming Pool
Depot
Beggar's Bridge
Thames Valley Athletic Centre
Colenorton Brook
The Timbralls
The Playing Fields
Fellow's Pond
Cemy
College
Eton College
Works
ETON
Recreation Ground
The Home Park
(Public Recreation Ground)
Victoria Bridge
South Meadow
Romney Island
Cutlers Ait
The Brocas
R. THAMES
Firework Ait
Windsor Bri
WINDSOR & ETON RIVERSIDE
Broad Water
Alexandra Gardens
The Goswells (N.T.)
Coach Park
WINDSOR & ETON CENTRAL
WINDSOR CASTLE
East Lawn
WINDSOR
South Slopes
Royal Mews
Golf Course
Cambridge Gate
The Home Park
Victoria Barracks
Offices
Cricket Ground
Frogmore Cottage
Frogmore
Frogmore House
Royal Mausoleum
Prince Consort Home Farm
Princess Margaret Hospital
River

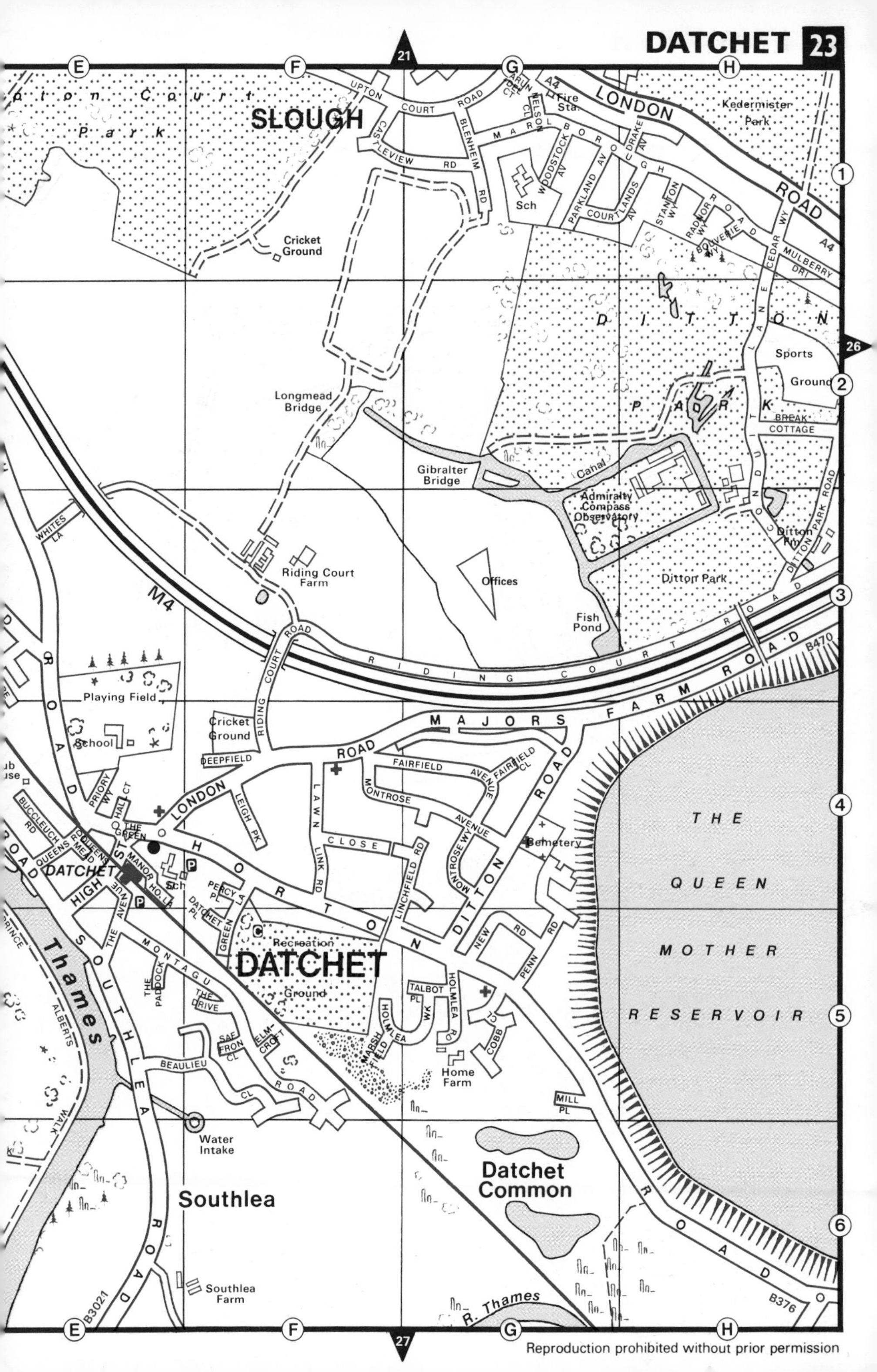
SLOUGH
Upton Court Park
UPTON COURT ROAD
CASTLEVIEW RD
BLENHEIM RD
LONDON ROAD
Fire Sta.
Kedermister Park
MARLBOROUGH ROAD
WOODSTOCK AV
PARKLAND AV
COURTLANDS AV
DRAKE AV
STANTON WY
RADNOR WY
BOUVERIE WY
CEDAR WY
MULBERRY DRI
A4
Sch
Cricket Ground
DITTON PARK
Sports Ground
BREAK COTTAGE
DITTON PARK ROAD
Longmead Bridge
Gibralter Bridge
Canal
Admiralty Compass Observatory
Ditton Fm
Ditton Park
Offices
Fish Pond
Riding Court Farm
M4
WHITES LA
RIDING COURT ROAD
MAJORS FARM ROAD
B470
Playing Field
School
Cricket Ground
DEEPFIELD
PRIORY WY
HALL CT
THE GREEN
LONDON ROAD
LEIGH PK
LAWN LINK RD
CLOSE
FAIRFIELD AVENUE
FAIRFIELD CL
MONTROSE AVENUE
MONTROSE WY
LINCHFIELD RD
DITTON ROAD
Cemetery
THE QUEEN MOTHER RESERVOIR
BUCCLEUCH RD
QUEENS MEAD
QUEENS RD
DATCHET
HIGH ST
MANOR HO. LA
Sch
HORTON ROAD
PERCY PL
DATCHET PL
GREEN LA
THE AVENUE
NEW RD
PENN RD
DATCHET
Recreation Ground
MONTAGU ROAD
THE PADDOCK
THE DRIVE
SAFFRON CL
ELMCROFT
TALBOT PL
HOLMLEA WK
HOLMLEA RD
MARSH FIELD
COBB CL
Home Farm
MILL PL
Thames
SOUTHLEA ROAD
ALBERTS WALK
BEAULIEU CL
Water Intake
Southlea
Datchet Common
Southlea Farm
R. Thames
B3021
B376
ROAD

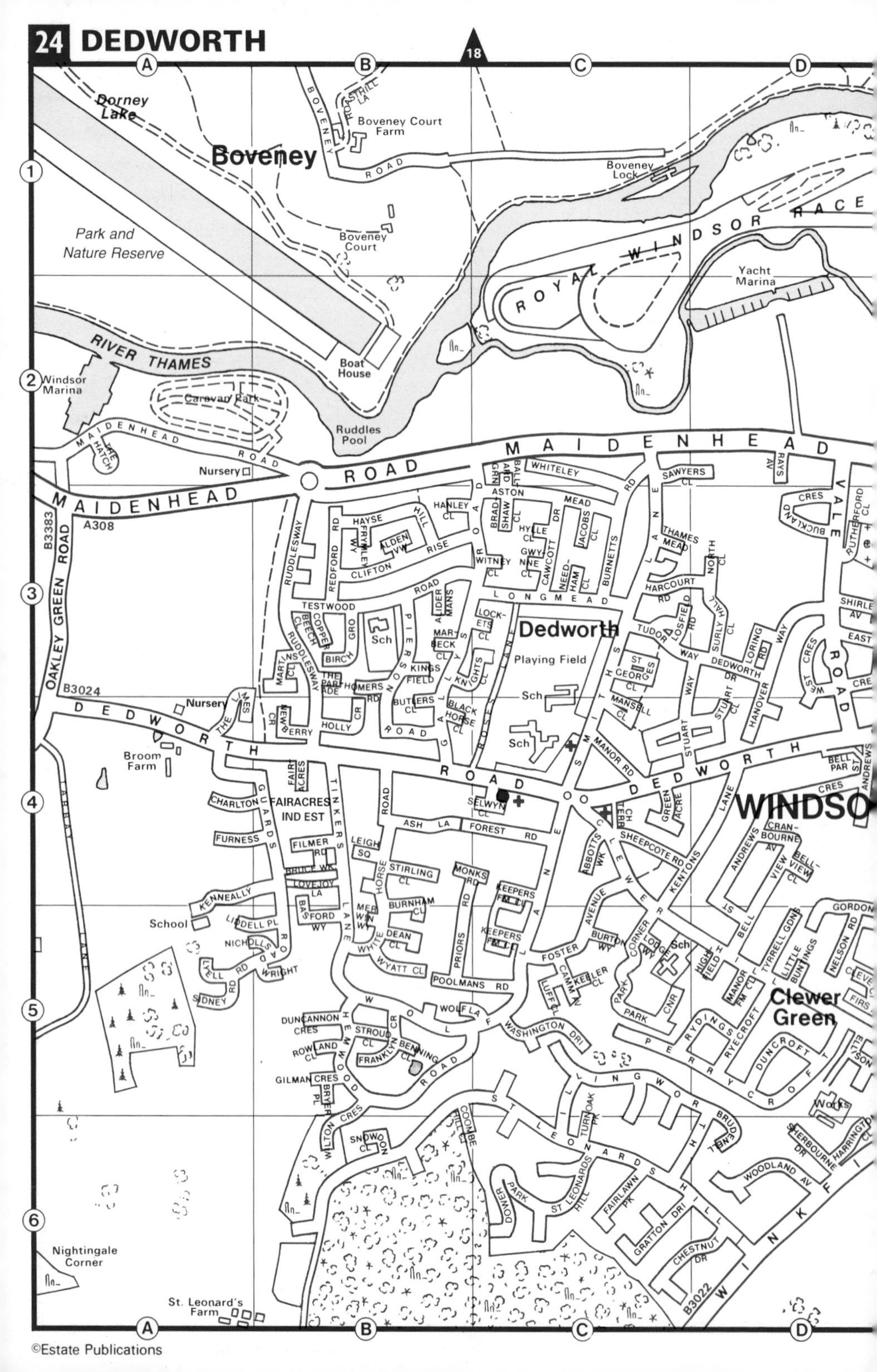

Dorney Lake
Boveney
Boveney Court Farm
Boveney Court
Park and Nature Reserve
RIVER THAMES
Windsor Marina
Caravan Park
Boat House
Ruddles Pool
Boveney Lock
ROYAL WINDSOR RACE
Yacht Marina
MAIDENHEAD ROAD
A308
B3383
OAKLEY GREEN ROAD
B3024
DEDWORTH ROAD
Dedworth
Playing Field
Broom Farm
FAIRACRES IND EST
WINDSO
Clewer Green
School
Nightingale Corner
St. Leonard's Farm
B3022
WINKFIELD

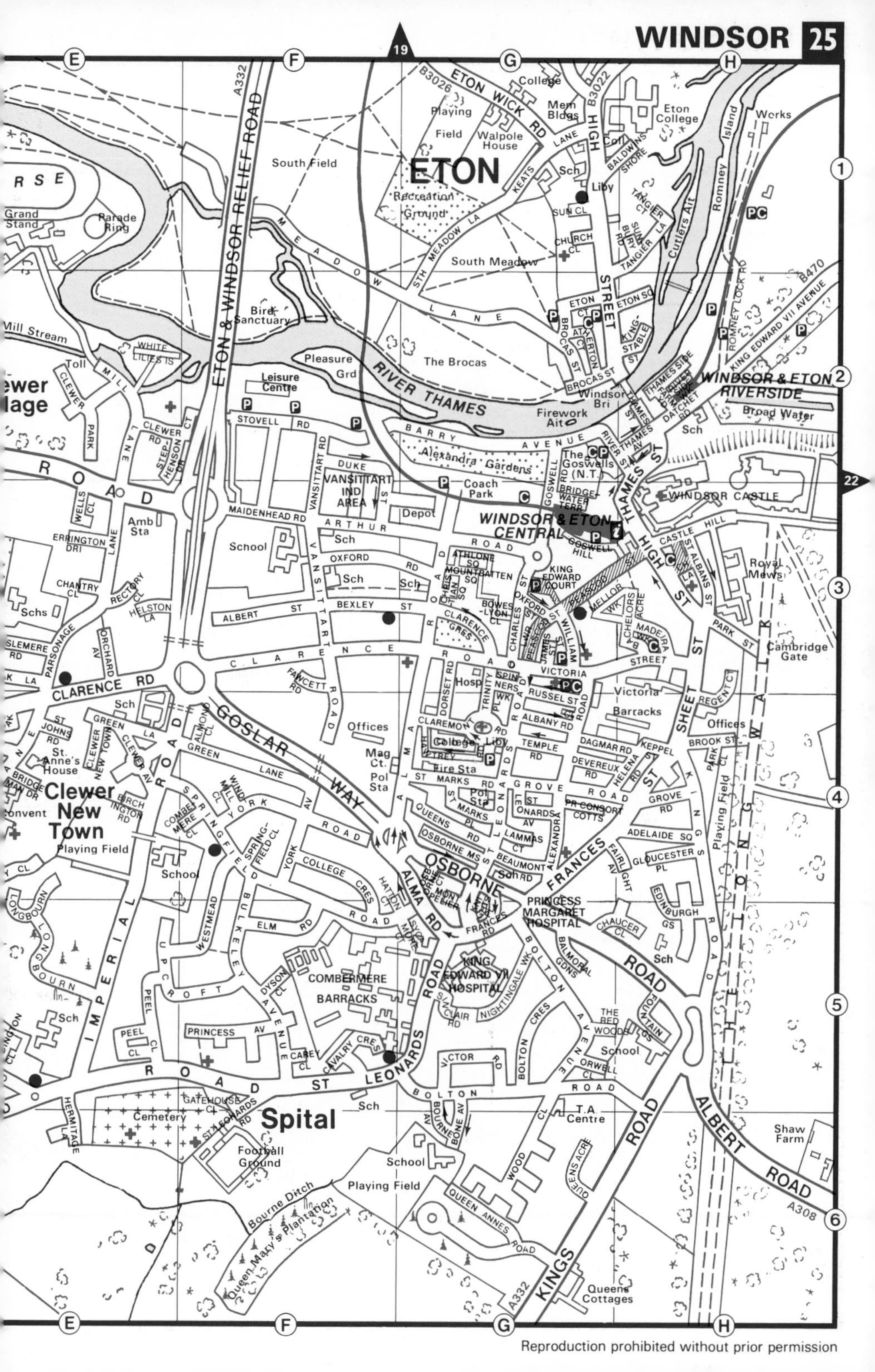
ETON
WINDSOR & ETON CENTRAL
WINDSOR & ETON RIVERSIDE
WINDSOR CASTLE
RIVER THAMES
ETON & WINDSOR RELIEF ROAD
A332
B3026
B3022
B470
A308
College
Eton College
ETON WICK RD
Mem Bldgs
Playing Field
Walpole House
South Field
Recreation Ground
South Meadow
MEADOW LANE
STH MEADOW LA
KEATS LANE
HIGH STREET
BALDWINS SHORE
TANGIER LA
Cutlers Ait
Romney Island
Works
Grand Stand
Parade Ring
Bird Sanctuary
Mill Stream
WHITE LILIES IS
Toll
Pleasure Grd
The Brocas
BROCAS ST
Windsor Bri
Firework Ait
Broad Water
Leisure Centre
STOVELL RD
BARRY AVENUE
Alexandra Gardens
The Goswells (N.T.)
Coach Park
VANSITTART IND AREA
DUKE ST
Depot
MAIDENHEAD RD
ARTHUR ROAD
OXFORD RD
BEXLEY ST
ALBERT ST
CLARENCE ROAD
CLARENCE RD
GOSLAR WAY
KING EDWARD COURT
PEASCOD ST
WILLIAM ST
VICTORIA STREET
Victoria Barracks
Royal Mews
Cambridge Gate
PARK ST
SHEET ST
KINGS RD
THE LONG WALK
Offices
Mag Ct.
Pol Sta
Hosp
College
Fire Sta
ST MARKS RD
GROVE ROAD
FRANCES ROAD
OSBORNE RD
ALMA RD
PRINCESS MARGARET HOSPITAL
KING EDWARD VII HOSPITAL
COMBERMERE BARRACKS
Clewer New Town
Clewer Village
Playing Field
School
IMPERIAL ROAD
ST LEONARDS ROAD
Spital
Cemetery
Football Ground
Bourne Ditch
Queen Mary's Plantation
QUEEN ANNES ROAD
T.A. Centre
KINGS ROAD
ALBERT ROAD
Shaw Farm
Queens Cottages
1
2
3
4
5
6
E
F
G
H
19
22

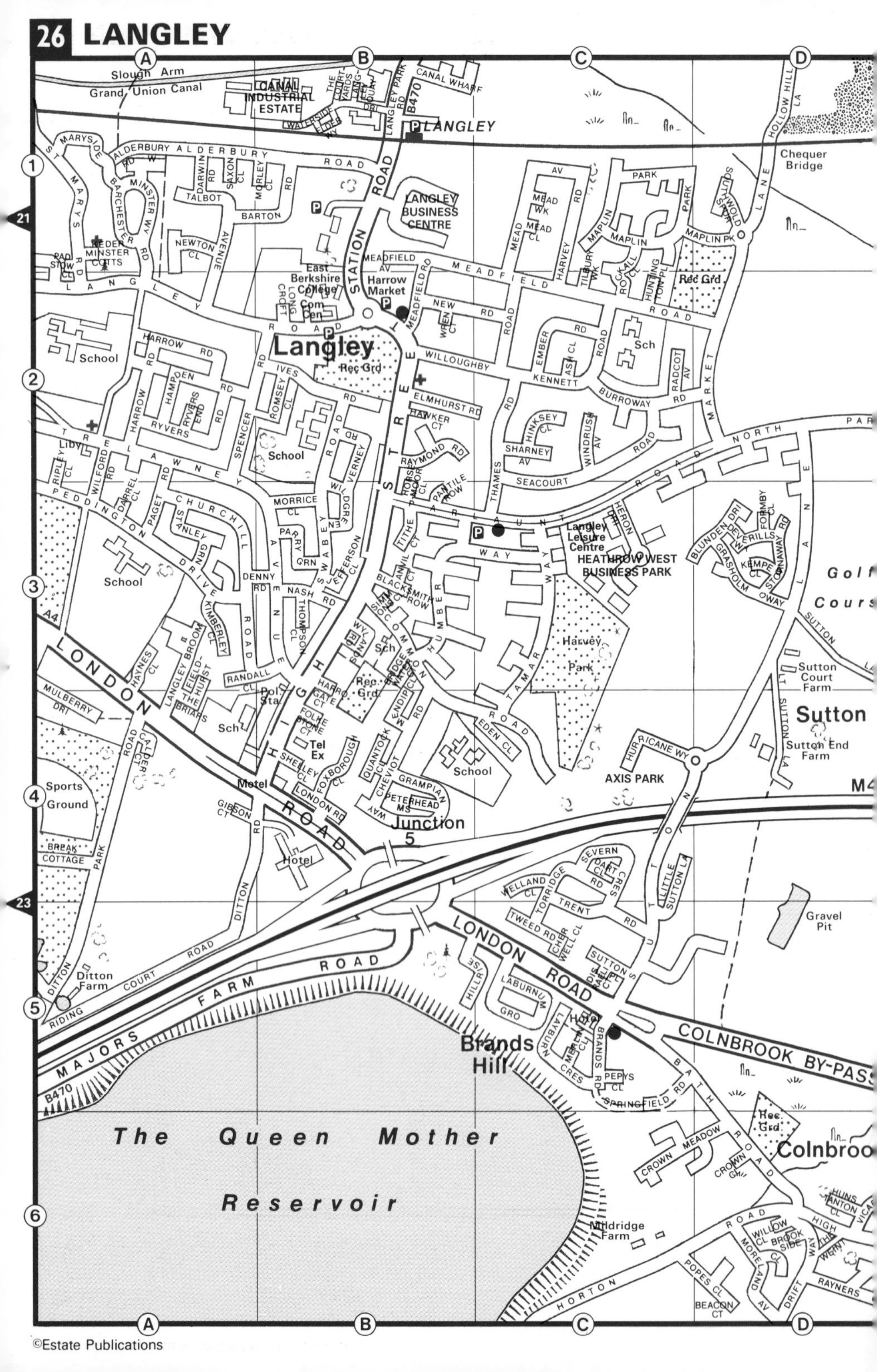

Slough Arm
Grand Union Canal
CANAL INDUSTRIAL ESTATE
CANAL WHARF
LANGLEY PARK RD
B470
LANGLEY
Chequer Bridge
HOLLOW HILL LA
ALDERBURY ROAD
ST MARYS RD
BARCHESTER RD
MINSTER WY
DARWIN RD
SAXON CL
MORLEY CL
TALBOT AV
BARTON RD
NEWTON CL
AVENUE
STATION ROAD
LANGLEY BUSINESS CENTRE
MEAD AV
MEAD WK
MEAD CL
HARVEY RD
PARK RD
MAPLIN PARK
MAPLIN PK
MARKET LANE
Rec Grd
PADSTOW CL
BEDER MINSTER COTTS
LANGLEY ROAD
LONG CROFT
East Berkshire College
Com Cen
Harrow Market
MEADFIELD AV
MEADFIELD RD
MEADFIELD ROAD
NEW RD
WREN CT
THAMES RD
EMBER RD
ASH CL
Sch
RADCOT AV
Langley
Rec Grd
School
HARROW RD
HAMPDEN RD
RYVERS RD
RYVERS END
IVES RD
ROMSEY CL
WILLOUGHBY RD
KENNETT RD
BURROWAY RD
ELMHURST RD
HAWKER CT
HINKSEY CL
SHARNEY AV
WINDRUSH AV
Liby
TRELAWNEY AVE
SPENCER RD
School
VERNEY RD
RAYMOND RD
SEACOURT RD
NORTH PARK
RIPLEY CL
WILFORD RD
DARREL CL
PAGET RD
HIGH STREET
HORSEMOOR CL
PANTILE ROW
PEDDINGTON CL
CHURCHILL RD
STANLEY GRN
MORRICE CL
WILDGREEN
PARLAUNT ROAD
PARLAUNT WAY
Langley Leisure Centre
HEATHROW WEST BUSINESS PARK
FORMBY CL
DEVERILLS WY
BLUNDEN DRI
GRASHOLM WAY
KEMPE CL
STONAWAY
Golf Course
School
DRIVE
PARRY GRN
DENNY RD
NASH RD
JEFFERSON CL
TITHE CT
ANVIL CT
BLACKSMITH ROW
HUMBER WAY
TAMAR WAY
Harvey Park
A4
LONDON ROAD
KIMBERLEY CL
THOMPSON CL
Sch
Rec Grd
SUTTON LANE
Sutton Court Farm
Sutton
Sutton End Farm
HAYNES CL
LANGLEY BROOM
FIELDHURST
THE BRIARS
RANDALL CL
Pol Sta
HARROGATE CT
MULBERRY DRI
Sch
FOLKESTONE CT
Tel Ex
SHELLEY CL
LONDON RD
FOXBOROUGH CL
QUANTOCK CL
CHEVIOT WAY
GRAMPIAN
PETERHEAD MS
MENDIP CL
EDEN CL
ROAD
School
HURRICANE WY
AXIS PARK
M4
Sports Ground
CALDER CT
Motel
GIBSON CT
Junction 5
BREAK COTTAGE
Hotel
DITTON PARK
DITTON ROAD
SEVERN CRES
WELLAND CL
TORRIDGE RD
DART CL
TRENT RD
LITTLE SUTTON LA
TWEED RD
CHERWELL CL
Gravel Pit
LONDON ROAD
HILLRISE
LABURNUM GRO
SUTTON PL
Ditton Farm
RIDING COURT ROAD
MAJORS FARM ROAD
B470
Hotel
LAYBURN CRES
MERLIN CL
BRANDS RD
Brands Hill
COLNBROOK BY-PASS
PEPYS CL
SPRINGFIELD RD
BATH ROAD
Rec Grd
Colnbrook
The Queen Mother Reservoir
CROWN MEADOW
CROWN
HUNSTANTON CL
Mildridge Farm
WILLOW CL
BROOKSIDE
MORELAND AV
HIGH ST
POPES CL
BEACON CT
HORTON ROAD
DRIFT WAY
RAYNERS
THE WEIR

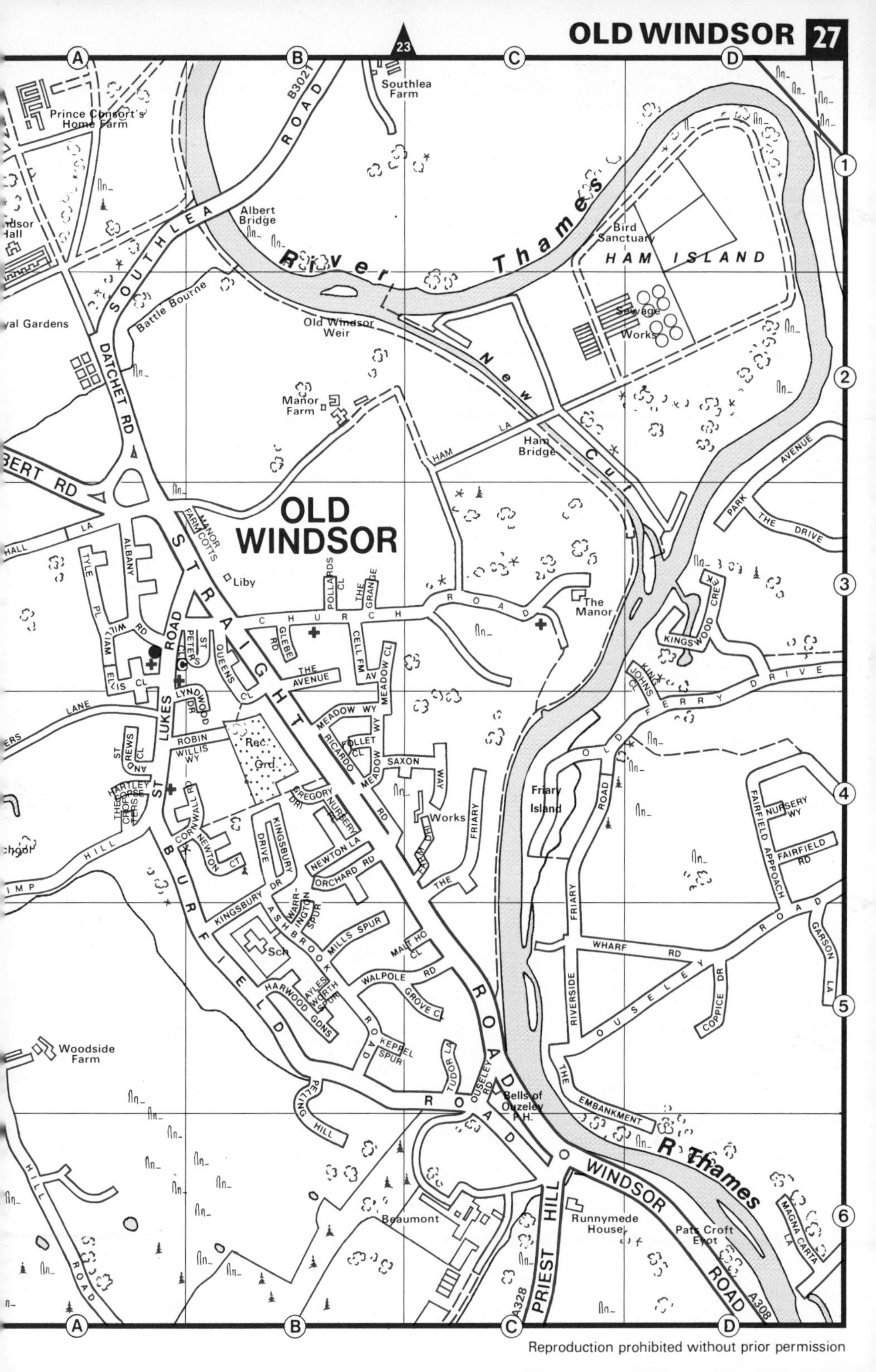
23
A
B
C
D
1
2
3
4
5
6
Southlea Farm
Prince Consort's Home Farm
B3021
SOUTHLEA ROAD
Albert Bridge
River Thames
Bird Sanctuary
HAM ISLAND
Sewage Works
Battle Bourne
Old Windsor Weir
New Cut
Manor Farm
HAM LA
Ham Bridge
DATCHET RD
ALBERT RD
OLD WINDSOR
MANOR FARM COTTS
STRAIGHT ROAD
Liby
POLLARDS CL
THE GRANGE
CHURCH ROAD
The Manor
PARK AVENUE
THE DRIVE
KINGSWOOD CREEK
KING JOHNS CL
OLD FERRY DRIVE
HALL LA
TYLE PL
ALBANY RD
WILLIAM CL
ELVIS CL
ST PETERS CL
QUEENS CL
GLEBE RD
THE AVENUE
CELL FM AV
MEADOW CL
MEADOW WY
LYNDWOOD DR
LANE
ST LUKES ROAD
ROBIN WILLIS WY
Rec. Grd.
RICARDO
FOLLET CL
SAXON WAY
ST ANDREWS CL
HARTLEY CL
THE CROFT
CORSE LAWN
CORNWALL RD
GREGORY DR
NURSERY RD
MEADOW RD
Works
FARM DR
THE FRIARY
Friary Island
OLD ROAD
FAIRFIELD APPROACH
NURSERY WY
FAIRFIELD RD
HILL
NEWTON CT
KINGSBURY DRIVE
NEWTON LA
ORCHARD RD
BURFIELD
KINGSBURY DR
ASHBROOK
WARRINGTON SPUR
MILLS SPUR
MALT HO CL
Sch
WALPOLE RD
GROVE CL
HARWOOD GDNS
AYLESWORTH SPUR
FRIARY
WHARF RD
OUSELEY ROAD
RIVERSIDE
COPPICE DR
GARSON LA
Woodside Farm
KEPPEL SPUR
TUDOR LA
OUSELEY RD
PELLING HILL
Bells of Ouzeley P.H.
THE EMBANKMENT
R. Thames
WINDSOR ROAD
PRIEST HILL
Runnymede House
Pats Croft Eyot
MAGNA CARTA LA
Beaumont
A328
A308
HILL ROAD
Royal Gardens
Windsor Hall
School
IMP
ERS

A - Z INDEX TO STREETS
with Postcodes

SLOUGH, WINDSOR, MAIDENHEAD

awcott Dri. SL4 24 C3
ecil Way. SL2 11 E4
edar Chase. SL6 9 F3
edar Way. SL3 23 H1
edars Rd. SL6 8 C5
entral Dri. SL1 19 E1
halgrove Clo. SL6 16 C1
hallow Ct. SL6 7 H3
halvey Gdns. SL1 20 C5
halvey Gro. SL1 19 H4
halvey Pk. SL1 20 C5
halvey Rd East. SL1 20 B5
halvey Rd West. SL1 20 B5
nantry Clo. SL4 25 E3
hapel La. SL2 13 F2
hapel St. SL1 20 C5
hapels Clo. SL1 19 E2
harles Gdns. SL2 21 E2
harles St. SL4 25 G3
harlotte Av. SL2 20 C2
harlton. SL4 24 A4
harlton Clo. SL1 19 G3
harter Rd. SL1 19 E1
hatfield. SL2 11 F5
hatsworth Clo. SL6 15 G1
haucer Clo. SL4 25 G5
hauntry Clo. SL6 8 D6
hauntry Rd. SL6 8 D6
heniston Grn. SL6 6 D5
herington Gate. SL6 7 F3
herry Av. SL3 21 G5
herry Garden La, White Waltham. SL6 14 D6
herry Garden La, Woolley Green. SL6 14 C4
herry Orchard. SL2 13 E1
herwell Clo, Brands Hill. SL3 26 C5
herwell Clo, Maidenhead. SL6 8 B4
ester Rd. SL1 20 B1
estnut Av. SL3 21 H5
estnut Clo. SL6 8 D3
estnut Dri. SL4 24 D6
estnut Pk. SL6 17 F4
eveley Gdns. SL1 10 B2
eviot Clo. SL6 8 D6
eviot Rd. SL3 26 B4
ichester Ct. SL1 21 E5
iltern Clo. SL6 8 D6
iltern Rd. SL1 10 B5
ilwick Rd. SL2 11 F3
ristian Sq. SL4 25 G3
urch Clo. SL4 22 A3
urch Dri. SL6 16 D2
urch Gro. SL3 13 F6
urch La, Maidenhead. SL6 17 E2
urch La, Slough. SL2 21 F1
urch La, Stoke Poges. SL2 12 C5
urch La. SL4 25 H3
urch Rd, Maidenhead. SL6 16 D1
urch Rd, Slough. SL2 11 H3
urch St, Burnham. SL1 10 B4
urch St, Chalvey. SL1 20 A5
urch St, Slough. SL1 20 C5
urch Ter. SL4 24 C4
urch Vw. SL6 14 D6
urch Walk. SL1 10 B4
urchfield Mews. SL2 21 E1
urchill Rd. SL3 26 A3
penham Clo. SL1 19 F1
penham La. SL1 19 F1
ppers Meadow. SL6 8 D3
re Rd, Maidenhead. SL6 7 H6
re Rd, Taplow. SL6 10 B6
refield Clo. SL6 7 F3
refield Dri. SL6 7 E3
refield Rd. SL6 7 F4
remont Rd. SL4 25 G4
rence Cres. SL4 25 G3
rence Rd. SL4 25 F3
rendon Ct. SL2 21 E2
ares Pasture. SL1 10 B3
ments Clo. SL1 21 E5
ve Ct. SL4 24 D5
vehurst Clo. SL2 12 D1
veland Clo. SL6 8 D6
wer Av. SL4 25 E4
wer Ct Rd. SL4 25 E2
wer Hill Rd. SL4 24 C4
wer New Town. SL4 25 E4
wer Pk. SL4 25 E2
Clewer Rd. SL4 25 E2
Clifton Clo. SL6 16 B2
Clifton Rise. SL4 24 B3
Clifton Rd. SL1 21 E5
Clive Ct. SL1 20 A5
Cliveden Mead. SL6 8 D2
Cliveden Rd. SL6 9 F3
Clivemont Rd. SL6 8 A4
Clonmel Way. SL1 10 B3
Coalmans Way. SL6 10 A5
Cobb Clo. SL3 23 G5
Cobblers Clo. SL2 11 G2
Cobham Clo. SL1 19 E2
Cockett Rd. SL3 21 H5
Coe Spur. SL1 19 G4
Coftards. SL2 21 G2
Colenorton Cres. SL4 19 E5
Colin Way. SL1 19 G4
College Av, Maidenhead. SL6 8 A5
College Av, Slough. SL1 20 B5
College Cres. SL4 25 F4
College Glen. SL6 7 H5
College Rise. SL6 7 H5
College Rd, Maidenhead. SL6 7 H5
College Rd, Slough. SL1 19 E2
Collier Clo. SL6 8 B3
Coln Clo. SL6 8 B4
Colnbrook By-Pass. SL3 26 C5
Colonial Rd. SL1 21 E4
Combemere Clo. SL4 25 F4
Common La. SL1 22 A2
Common Rd, Dorney. SL4 18 C5
Common Rd, Eaton Wick. SL4 19 F5
Common Rd, Langley. SL3 26 B3
Compton Dri. SL6 7 E4
Concorde Rd. SL6 15 H2
Concorde Way. SL1 19 H3
Conduit La. SL3 23 H3
Conegar Ct. SL1 20 B4
Coniston Cres. SL1 10 C5
Connaught Clo. SL6 8 A3
Connaught Rd. SL1 21 E4
Conningsby Clo. SL6 15 H3
Convent Rd. SL4 24 D4
Conway Rd. SL6 10 B6
Coombe Hill Ct. SL4 24 B6
Cooper Way. SL1 19 G3
Cope Ct. SL6 7 G5
Copper Beech Clo. SL4 24 B3
Copse Clo. SL1 19 F2
Copthorn Clo. SL6 15 E2
Cordwallis Rd. SL6 8 A4
Cordwallis St. SL6 8 A4
Corfe Gdns. SL1 19 F1
Corfe Pl. SL6 7 G5
Cornwall Av. SL2 11 H1
Cornwall Clo, Eaton Wick. SL4 19 E5
Cornwall Clo, Maidenhead. SL6 8 A2
Coronation Av. SL3 21 H1
Coronation Rd. SL6 14 A1
Cotswold Clo. SL1 19 H4
Coulson Way. SL1 10 A5
Court Cres. SL1 20 B1
Court Clo. SL6 17 E4
Court Dri. SL6 9 E1
Court La, Burnham. SL1 10 C3
Court La, Slough. SL1 18 A4
Court Rd. SL6 9 E2
Courtfield Dri. SL6 7 G6
Courthouse Rd. SL6 7 G5
Courtlands. SL6 8 B6
Courtlands Av. SL3 23 G1
Coverdale Way. SL2 11 E4
Cowper Rd. SL2 11 G4
Cox Green La. SL6 15 F3
Cox Green Rd. SL6 15 G2
Cranbourne Av. SL4 24 D4
Cranbourne Clo. SL1 19 H2
Cranbourne Rd. SL1 19 H2
Cranbrook Dri. SL6 7 F3
Craufurd Rise. SL6 8 A4
Crayle St. SL2 11 G3
Creden Clo. SL6 7 H4
Crescent Dri. SL6 8 A5
Cress Rd. SL1 19 G3
Cresswells Mead. SL6 16 D5
Crofthill Rd. SL2 11 G4
Cromer Ct. SL1 20 C2
Cromwell Dri. SL1 20 C1
Cromwell Rd. SL6 7 G5
Cross Oak. SL4 25 E4
Crosthwaite Way. SL1 10 C5
Crow Piece. SL2 11 E2
Crown Clo. SL3 26 D6
Crown La, Farnham Royal. SL2 11 G2
Crown La, Maidenhead. SL6 8 C5
Crown Meadow. SL3 26 C6
Crummock Clo. SL1 10 B5
Culham Dri. SL6 8 A2
Culley Way. SL6 15 E2
Cumberland Av. SL2 11 H4
Cumbrae Clo. SL2 21 E3
Cumbria Clo. SL6 15 G2
Curls La. SL6 16 A2
Curls Rd. SL6 15 H2

Dagmar Rd. SL4 25 G4
Damson Gro. SL1 20 A5
Dandridge Clo. SL3 21 G6
Darlings La. SL6 6 D3
Darrel Clo. SL3 26 A3
Dart Clo. SL3 26 C4
Darvills La. SL1 20 B5
Darwin Rd. SL3 26 A1
Dashwood Clo. SL3 21 F6
Datchet Pl. SL3 23 F5
Datchet Rd, Slough. SL3 20 D6
Datchet Rd, Windsor. SL4 25 H2
Dawes East Rd. SL1 10 C3
Dawes Moor Clo. SL2 21 G2
Dawson Clo. SL4 25 E4
Deal Av. SL1 11 E6
Dean Clo. SL4 24 B5
Deans Clo. SL2 13 F3
Deansfield Clo. SL6 7 G2
Decies Way. SL2 12 D2
Dedworth Dri. SL4 24 D3
Dedworth Rd. SL4 24 C4
Deena Clo. SL1 19 E1
Deepfield. SL3 23 F4
Deerswood. SL6 8 C4
Denham Clo. SL6 7 G6
Denmark St. SL6 8 A4
Dennis Way. SL1 18 D1
Denny Rd. SL3 26 A3
Depot Rd. SL6 8 B6
Derek Rd. SL6 8 D4
Derwent Dri, Maidenhead. SL6 7 H4
Derwent Dri, Slough. SL1 10 C5
Desborough Cres. SL6 15 G1
Devereux Rd. SL4 25 G4
Deverills Way. SL3 26 D3
Devon Av. SL1 20 A1
Devonshire Clo. SL2 11 G2
Devonshire Gdns. SL2 11 G2
Dhoon Rise. SL6 16 B1
Diamond Rd. SL1 21 E4
Diana Clo. SL3 21 H2
Disraeli Ct. SL3 26 C5
Ditton Park Rd. SL3 26 A5
Ditton Rd, Datchet. SL3 23 G5
Ditton Rd, Langley. SL3 26 A5
Doddsfield Rd. SL2 11 F3
Dolphin Rd. SL1 21 E4
Donnington Gdns. SL6 8 B3
Dorchester Clo. SL6 7 F3
Dornels. SL2 21 F2
Dorney Reach Rd. SL6 17 G3
Dorney Wood Rd. SL1 10 B1
Dorset Rd. SL4 25 G4
Douglas Rd. SL2 12 B6
Dove House Cres. SL2 10 D3
Dover Rd. SL1 11 F6
Dower Pk. SL4 24 C6
Downs Rd. SL3 21 G5
Drake Av. SL3 23 H1
Drift Way. SL3 26 D6
Dropmore Rd. SL1 10 B1
Duchess St. SL1 19 E2
Dudley Ct. SL1 20 D6
Duffield La. SL2 12 C1
Duffield Pk. SL2 12 D5
Duke St. SL4 25 F2
Dunbar Clo. SL2 21 E2
Duncannon Cres. SL4 24 B5
Duncroft. SL4 24 D5
Dundee Rd. SL1 11 F5
Dungrove Hill La. SL6 6 A2
Dunholme End. SL6 15 H3
Dunster Gdns. SL1 19 F1
Dupre Clo. SL1 18 D3
Durham Av. SL1 11 F6
Dutch Elm Av. SL4 22 D4
Dyson Clo. SL4 25 F5

Earls La. SL1 19 E2
Earlsfield. SL6 16 D5
East Burnham La. SL2 11 F1
East Cres. SL4 24 D3
East Rd. SL6 8 A5
Eastbourne Rd. SL1 11 F6
Eastcroft. SL2 11 G4
Eastfield Clo. SL1 20 D5
Eastfield Rd. SL1 10 A5
Ebsworth Clo. SL6 9 E2
Eden Clo. SL3 26 C4
Edinburgh Av. SL1 11 F5
Edinburgh Gdns. SL4 25 H5
Edinburgh Rd. SL6 8 A3
Edith Rd. SL6 7 E5
Edmunds Way. SL2 21 F1
Egerton Rd. SL2 11 E4
Egremont Gdns. SL1 19 F2
Eight Acres. SL1 10 B3
Elder Way. SL3 26 B1
Elderfield Rd. SL2 12 C1
Elizabeth Way. SL2 12 C3
Elliman Av. SL2 20 C2
Ellington Gdns. SL6 9 E5
Ellington Pk. SL6 8 A3
Ellington Rd. SL6 9 E5
Ellis Av. SL1 20 B4
Ellison Clo. SL4 24 D5
Elm Clo. SL2 12 A1
Elm Gro. SL6 8 A5
Elm Rd. SL4 25 F5
Elmar Grn. SL2 11 F3
Elmcroft. SL3 23 F5
Elmhurst Rd. SL3 26 B2
Elmshott La. SL1 18 D1
Elmwood. SL6 8 D1
Elmwood Rd. SL2 21 E3
Eltham Av. SL1 19 E2
Elton Dri. SL6 7 H4
Ely Av. SL1 20 A1
Ember Rd. SL3 26 C2
Emerald Ct. SL1 20 C5
Ennerdale Cres. SL1 10 C5
Erica Clo. SL1 18 D1
Errington Dri. SL4 25 E3
Eskdale Gdns. SL6 16 D5
Essex Av. SL2 11 H5
Eton Clo. SL3 22 D3
Eton Ct. SL4 22 A3
Eton Rd. SL3 22 D2
Eton Sq. SL4 22 B3
Eton Wick Rd. SL4 19 E5
Eton and Windsor Relief Rd. SL4 25 F2
Evenlode. SL6 8 B4
Everard Av. SL1 20 B4
Eyre Grn. SL2 11 F3

Fair Acre. SL6 7 G6
Fairacres. SL4 24 B4
Faircroft. SL2 11 G4
Fairfield Av. SL3 23 F4
Fairfield Clo. SL3 23 G4
Fairfield La. SL2 11 H1
Fairfield Rd. SL1 10 B3
Fairford Rd. SL6 8 A4
Fairlawn Pl. SL4 24 C6
Fairlea. SL6 15 F3
Fairlie Rd. SL1 11 F6
Fairlight Av. SL4 25 G4
Fairview Rd, Slough. SL2 11 E4
Fairview Rd, Taplow. SL6 10 A5
Falmouth Rd. SL1 11 F6
Fane Way. SL6 15 H1
Faraday Clo. SL2 11 H4
Faraday Rd. SL2 11 G5
Farm Clo, Holyport. SL6 16 D5
Farm Clo, Maidenhead. SL6 7 E5
Farm Cres. SL2 21 F1
Farm La. SL1 20 B2
Farm Rd, Maidenhead. SL6 7 E5
Farm Rd, Taplow. SL6 10 A6
Farm Yd. SL4 25 H2
Farmers Clo. SL6 15 E2
Farmers Way. SL6 15 E2
Farnburn Av. SL1 11 H5
Farnham La. SL2 11 E3
Farnham Park La. SL2 12 A2
Farnham Rd. SL1 11 H3
Farthing Green La. SL2 12 D3
Fawcett Rd. SL4 25 F3
Fawley Clo. SL6 7 H2
Fern Dri. SL6 10 A6
Fernley Ct. SL6 7 H3
Ferrers Clo. SL1 18 D2
Ferry Rd. SL6 17 E2
Fieldhurst. SL3 26 A3
Fielding Gdns. SL3 21 F5
Fielding Rd. SL6 7 F5
Fifield Rd. SL6 17 F6
Filey Spur. SL1 19 G3
Filmer Rd. SL4 24 B4
Finch Ct. SL6 15 H1
Fir Tree Av. SL2 12 C5
Firs Av. SL4 24 D5
Firs La. SL6 14 D2
First Cres. SL1 20 A1
Fishery Rd. SL6 16 D1
Fishguard Spur. SL1 21 E5
Flamborough Spur. SL1 19 F3
Fleetwood Rd. SL2 20 D3
Florence Av. SL6 8 B4
Foliejohn Way. SL6 14 D4
Folkestone Ct. SL3 26 B4
Fontwell Clo. SL6 7 E4
Forest Rd. SL4 24 C4
Forlease Clo. SL6 8 C6
Forlease Dri. SL6 8 C6
Forlease Rd. SL6 8 C5
Formby Clo. SL6 26 D3
Forsythia Gdns. SL3 21 H5
Foster Av. SL4 24 C5
Fosters Path. SL2 11 E4
Fotherby Ct. SL6 8 C6
Fotheringay Gdns. SL1 19 F1
Fountain Gdns. SL4 25 H5
Fox Rd. SL3 21 G6
Foxborough Clo. SL3 26 B4
Foxherne. SL3 21 F5
Framewood Rd. SL2 13 F2
France Av. SL6 8 D4
Frances Rd. SL4 25 G5
Frances St. SL4 25 G4
Francis Way. SL1 18 C1
Frank Sutton Way. SL1 20 A3
Franklin Av. SL2 11 G4
Franklyn Cres. SL4 24 B5
Frascati Way. SL6 8 B5
*Fraunchies Ct, Pool La. SL1 20 B3
Freemans Clo. SL2 12 D1
Frenchum Gdns. SL1 19 E1
Frogmore Clo. SL1 19 G3
Frogmore Dri. SL4 22 B5
Frymley Way. SL4 24 B3
Fullbrook Clo. SL6 8 C4
Fullers Yard. SL6 8 D2
Fulmer Common Rd. SL3 13 H1
Furness. SL4 24 A4
Furnival Av. SL2 11 G5
Furrow Way. SL6 15 E2
Furze Platt Rd. SL6 7 E3
Furze Rd. SL6 7 H3
Furzen Clo. SL2 11 F3

Gables Clo, Datchet. SL3 23 E3
Gables Clo, Maidenhead. SL6 8 D4
Gage Clo. SL6 16 A2
Gainsborough Dri. SL6 15 H3
Galahad Clo. SL1 19 G3
Galleons La. SL2 13 G4
Galloway Chase. SL2 20 D3
Gallys Rd. SL4 24 B4
Galvin Rd. SL2 19 H2
Garden Clo. SL6 15 E1
Garden Mews. SL1 20 C3
Gardner Rd. SL6 8 A2
Garnet Clo. SL1 19 F3
Garrard Rd. SL2 11 E4
Garthlands. SL6 7 H2
Gas La. SL6 16 C3
Gascons Gro. SL2 11 G4
Gatehouse Clo. SL4 25 F5
Gatewick Clo. SL1 20 C4
Gatward Av. SL6 15 F3
Gaveston Rd. SL2 11 E3
Gays La. SL6 16 C6
George Green Rd. SL3 21 H2
Gerrards Cross Rd. SL2 12 D2
Gervaise Clo. SL1 19 E2
Gibson Ct. SL3 26 A4
Gilchrist Way. SL6 14 A1
Gilliat Rd. SL1 20 C3
Gilman Cres. SL4 24 B5
Gilmore Clo. SL3 21 F4

Gladstone Way. SL1 19 F2
Glanmor Rd. SL2 21 F3
Glasgow Rd. SL1 11 F5
Glebe Clo. SL6 17 G2
Glebe Rd. SL6 16 D1
Glenavon Gdns. SL3 21 G6
Glentworth Pl. SL1 19 H2
Gloucester Av. SL1 20 A1
Gloucester Pl. SL4 25 H4
Gloucester Rd. SL6 8 A3
Godolphin Rd. SL1 20 B2
Golden Ball La. SL6 7 E2
Goldsworthy Way. SL1 10 C6
Goodman Pk. SL2 21 F4
Goodwin Rd. SL2 11 F3
Goose Grn. SL2 11 G2
Gordon Rd,
 Maidenhead. SL6 7 G5
Gordon Rd,
 Windsor. SL4 24 D5
Gore Rd. SL1 10 A3
Gorsemeade. SL1 19 G2
Goslar Way. SL4 25 F4
Gosling Grn. SL3 21 H6
Gosling Rd. SL3 21 H5
Goswell Hill. SL4 25 G3
Goswell Rd. SL4 25 G3
Gowings Grn. SL1 19 E3
Grace Ct. SL1 20 A3
Grafton Clo,
 George Green. SL3 21 H2
Grafton Clo,
 Maidenhead. SL6 8 A2
Graham Clo. SL6 15 G1
Grampian Way. SL3 26 B4
Grangewood. SL3 21 F1
Grant Av. SL1 20 C2
Granville Av. SL2 20 A1
Grasholme Way. SL3 26 D3
Grasmere Av. SL2 20 D3
Grassy La. SL6 7 H5
Gratton Dri. SL4 24 C6
Grays All. SL6 6 D5
Grays Park Rd. SL2 12 D4
Grays Pl. SL2 20 C3
Grays Rd. SL1 20 C3
Great Hill Cres. SL6 15 F1
Green Acre. SL4 24 C4
Green Clo,
 Maidenhead. SL6 8 B3
Green Clo,
 Taplow. SL6 10 A6
Green La,
 Burnham. SL1 10 C3
Green La,
 Datchet. SL3 23 F5
Green La,
 Littlewick Grn. SL6 14 A1
Green La,
 Maidenhead. SL6 8 C6
Green La,
 Windsor. SL4 25 E4
Greendale Mews. SL2 20 D3
Greenfern Av. SL1 10 C6
Greenfields. SL6 16 B1
Greenock Rd. SL1 11 F6
Greenside. SL2 11 G5
Greenway. SL1 10 B2
Greenways Dri. SL6 7 E4
Grenfell Av. SL6 8 B6
Grenfell Pl. SL6 8 B6
Grenfell Rd. SL6 8 A5
Grenville Clo. SL1 10 B2
Gresham Rd. SL1 11 G6
Greystoke Rd. SL2 11 E5
Griffin Clo,
 Maidenhead. SL6 16 A1
Griffin Clo,
 Slough. SL1 19 H3
Gringer Hill. SL6 7 H3
Grosvenor Dri. SL6 8 D4
Grove Clo. SL1 20 D5
Grove Rd,
 Maidenhead. SL6 8 B6
Grove Rd, Slough. SL1 10 D3
Grove Rd,
 Windsor. SL4 25 H4
Guards Rd. SL4 24 B4
Guards Club Rd. SL6 8 D5
Gwendale. SL6 7 G3
Gwent Clo. SL6 15 F2
Gwynne Clo. SL4 24 C3

Haddon Rd. SL6 15 G1
Hadlow Ct. SL1 19 H2
Hag Hill La. SL6 9 H5
Hag Hill Rise. SL6 9 H5
Haig Dri. SL1 19 G3
Half Meadow. SL1 10 B2

Halifax Clo. SL6 7 E4
Halifax Rd. SL6 7 E4
Halifax Way. SL6 7 E4
Halkingcroft. SL3 21 F5
Hall Ct. SL3 23 E4
Hall Place La. SL6 6 A5
Hambledon Walk. SL6 8 A2
Hamilton Gdns. SL1 10 A3
Hamilton Pk. SL6 7 E6
Hamilton Rd. SL1 11 F6
Hampden Clo. SL2 12 D4
Hampden Rd,
 Maidenhead. SL6 7 F4
Hampden Rd,
 Slough. SL3 26 A2
Hampshire Av. SL1 20 A1
Hanbury Clo. SL6 9 H4
Hanley Clo. SL4 24 B3
Hanover Clo. SL4 20 D6
Hanover Mead. SL6 17 E3
Hanover Way. SL4 24 D3
Harborough Clo. SL1 18 C2
Harcourt Clo. SL6 17 G3
Harcourt Rd,
 Dorney Reach. SL6 17 G3
Harcourt Rd,
 Windsor. SL4 24 C3
Hardwick Clo. SL6 7 E4
Hardy Clo. SL1 19 F2
Hare Shoots. SL6 16 A1
Harefield Rd. SL6 7 E5
Harewood Pl. SL1 21 E5
Hargrave Rd. SL6 7 H4
Harkness Rd. SL1 10 A5
Harrington Clo. SL4 24 D6
Harris Gdns. SL1 20 A4
Harrison Way. SL1 18 C2
Harrogate Ct. SL3 26 B3
Harrow Clo. SL6 8 A3
Harrow La. SL6 7 H3
Harrow Rd. SL3 26 A2
Hartland Clo. SL1 20 B4
Hartley Clo. SL3 13 F3
Harvest Hill Rd. SL6 16 A2
Harvey Rd. SL3 26 C2
Harwich Rd. SL1 11 F6
Haslemere Rd. SL4 25 E3
Hasting Clo. SL6 16 D4
Hatch La. SL4 24 D5
Hatchgate Gdns. SL1 10 C3
Hatfield Clo. SL6 7 G6
Hatfield Rd. SL1 20 D5
Hatton Av. SL2 12 A6
Hatton Ct. SL4 25 F4
Havelock Cres. SL6 7 F5
Havelock Rd. SL6 7 F5
Hawker Ct. SL3 26 B2
Hawkshill Rd. SL2 11 G3
Hawthorn Gdns. SL6 15 H2
Hawthorne Cres. SL1 20 C2
Hawtrey Clo. SL1 21 F5
Hawtrey Rd. SL4 25 G4
Haymill Rd. SL1 10 D4
Haynes Clo. SL3 26 A3
Hayse Hill. SL4 24 B3
Haywards Mead. SL4 19 F6
Hazelhurst Rd. SL1 10 C2
Hazell Clo. SL6 8 B4
Hazell Way. SL2 12 D1
Hazlemere Rd. SL2 21 E3
Headington Clo. SL6 7 E5
Headington Rd. SL6 7 E4
Hearne Dri. SL6 16 C5
Heathcote. SL6 16 D4
Heathlands Dri. SL6 7 E6
Hedingham Mews. SL6 7 H5
Helena Rd. SL4 25 H4
Helmsdale. SL6 7 F3
Helston La. SL4 25 E3
Hemming Way. SL2 11 G3
Hemson Av. SL6 21 F5
Hemwood Rd. SL4 24 B5
Hencroft St. SL1 20 D5
Hendons Way. SL6 16 D5
Henley Rd,
 Maidenhead. SL6 6 A2
Henley Rd, Slough. SL1 11 H6
Henry Rd. SL1 20 B4
Hermitage Clo. SL3 21 F5
Hermitage La. SL4 25 E5
Heron Dri. SL3 26 C3
Herschel St. SL1 20 C5
Hetherington Clo. SL2 11 E3
Hever Clo. SL6 7 G6
Heynes Grn. SL6 15 F3
Heywood Av. SL6 15 E5
Heywood Clo. SL6 15 E4
Hibbert Rd. SL6 16 C3
High St, Bray. SL6 17 E3

High St, Burnham. SL1 10 B3
High St, Chalvey. SL1 20 A5
High St,
 Colnbrook. SL3 26 D6
High St, Datchet. SL3 23 E4
High St, Eton. SL4 22 A3
High St, Langley. SL3 26 B4
High St,
 Maidenhead. SL6 8 B5
High St, Slough. SL1 20 D5
High St, Taplow. SL6 9 F3
High St, Windsor. SL4 25 H3
High Town Rd. SL6 8 A6
Highfield. SL4 24 D5
Highfield La. SL6 15 E2
Highfield Rd. SL6 7 F5
Highgrove Pk. SL6 8 A4
Highway Av. SL6 7 E5
Highway Rd. SL6 7 F6
Hill Farm Rd. SL6 9 F2
Hillary Rd. SL3 21 H5
Hillersdon. SL2 21 E1
Hillmead Ct. SL6 9 G4
Hillrise. SL3 26 B5
Hillside,
 Maidenhead. SL6 15 H1
Hillside,
 Slough. SL1 20 B5
Hilperton Rd. SL1 20 C4
Hindhay La. SL6 7 F2
Hinksey Clo. SL3 26 C2
Hinton Rd. SL1 19 E1
Hitcham La. SL6 9 F2
Hitcham Rd. SL6 9 H3
Hobbis Clo. SL6 7 E6
Hockley La. SL2 13 E2
Hogarth Clo. SL1 19 E1
Hogfair La. SL1 10 C3
Hollow Hill La. SL3 26 D1
Holly Cres. SL4 24 B4
Hollybush Hill. SL2 13 E1
Holman Leaze. SL6 8 B5
Holmedale. SL6 21 F2
Holmlea Rd. SL3 23 G5
Holmlea Walk. SL3 23 F5
Holmwood Clo. SL6 15 F1
Holyport Rd. SL6 16 C6
Holyport St. SL6 16 C6
Home Farm Way. SL3 13 F2
Home Meadow. SL2 11 H2
Homers Rd. SL4 24 B3
Homeside Clo. SL6 8 A2
Homestead Rd. SL6 15 H2
Homewood. SL3 21 G2
Hornbeam Gdns. SL1 20 D6
Horseguards Dri. SL6 8 C6
Horsemoor Clo. SL3 26 B3
Horton Clo. SL6 8 D3
Horton Rd,
 Colnbrook. SL3 26 C6
Horton Rd,
 Datchet. SL3 23 F4
Howard Av. SL2 12 B6
Howarth Rd. SL6 8 C6
Hubert Rd. SL3 21 H6
Hughenden Clo. SL6 7 G6
Hughenden Rd. SL1 20 B2
Hull Clo. SL1 19 H4
Humber Way. SL3 26 B3
Hungerford Av. SL2 12 B6
Hungerford Dri. SL6 8 A1
Hunstanton Clo. SL3 26 D6
Hunter Ct. SL1 10 B5
Huntercombe Clo. SL6 10 B6
Huntercombe La Nth.
 SL6 10 B5
Huntercombe La Sth.
 SL4 18 B2
Hunters Way. SL1 18 D3
Huntington Pl. SL3 26 C2
Hunts La. SL6 9 F2
Hurley La. SL6 6 A1
Hurricane Way. SL6 26 C4
Hurst Rd. SL1 10 D5
Hurstfield Dri. SL6 10 B6
Hurworth Rd. SL3 21 F6
Huxtable Gdns. SL6 17 F5
Hylle Clo. SL3 24 C3

Ilchester Clo. SL6 15 G1
Illingworth. SL4 24 C5
Imperial Rd. SL4 25 E5
In The Ray. SL6 8 A6
India Rd. SL1 21 E4

INDUSTRIAL & RETAIL:
Axis Park Ind Est. SL3 26 C4
Bath Rd Retail Pk. SL1 11 E6
Canal Ind Est. SL6 8 B1
Data Base. SL6 15 H2

Fairacres Ind Est. SL4 24 B4
Foundation Pk. SL6 14 D2
Furze Platt Ind Area.
 SL6 7 H2
Heathrow West
 Business Park. SL3 26 C3
Langley Business
 Centre. SL3 26 B1
Maidenhead Business
 Campus. SL6 14 C4
North Town Ind Est.
 SL6 8 A4
Priors Way Ind Est.
 SL6 16 C4
Progress Business
 Centre. SL1 10 D6
Slough Trading Est.
 SL1 11 G6
The Switchback
 Ind Area. SL6 7 H2
Vansittart Ind Area.
 SL4 25 F3
Vanwall Business Pk.
 SL6 15 G2
Westacott Business
 Centre. SL6 14 C4
Whitebrook Park
 Ind Est. SL6 8 D1
Inkerman Rd. SL4 19 E5
Institute Rd. SL6 9 G5
Iona Cres. SL1 10 D6
Ipswich Rd. SL1 11 F6
Islett Pk. SL6 9 E1
Islett Park Dri. SL6 9 E1
Islett Rd. SL6 8 D1
Ives Rd. SL3 26 B2
Ivy Cres. SL1 19 F1

Jacobs Clo. SL4 24 C3
James St. SL4 25 G3
Jefferson Clo. SL3 26 B3
Jellicoe Clo. SL1 19 G3
Jennery La. SL1 10 C3
John Taylor Ct. SL1 20 A4
Journeys End. SL2 12 C6
Jubilee Rd. SL6 14 A2
Juniper Ct. SL1 21 E5
Juniper Dri. SL6 8 D5

Kaywood Clo. SL3 21 G6
Keats La. SL4 25 G1
Keble Rd. SL6 7 H5
Kederminster Cotts.
 SL3 26 A1
Keel Dri. SL1 19 H3
Keeler Clo. SL4 24 C5
Keepers Farm Clo. SL4 24 C5
Kelpatrick Rd. SL1 10 D6
Kelsey Clo. SL6 15 H3
Kempe Clo. SL3 26 D3
Kemsley Chase. SL2 12 A2
Kendal Clo. SL2 20 D3
Kendal Dri. SL2 20 D3
Kendrick Rd. SL3 21 F6
Kenilworth Clo. SL1 20 D6
Kenneally. SL4 24 A4
Kennedy Clo. SL6 7 G6
Kennett Rd. SL3 26 C2
Kennet Rd. SL6 8 B5
Kent Av. SL1 11 H5
Kent Way. SL6 7 H3
Kentons La. SL4 24 C4
Kenwood Clo. SL6 7 E6
Keppel St. SL4 25 H4
Keswick Ct. SL2 20 D3
Keys La. SL6 8 B6
Kidderminster Rd. SL2 11 F2
Kidwells Clo. SL6 8 B5
Kiln Pl. SL6 7 E1
Kimber Clo. SL4 24 A3
Kimberley Clo. SL3 26 A3
Kimbers Dri. SL1 10 C3
Kimbers La. SL6 16 A3
King Edward Ct. SL4 25 G3
King Edward St. SL1 20 B5
King Edward VII Av.
 SL4 22 B4
King St. SL6 8 B6
Kinghorn La. SL6 7 H2
Kinghorn Pk. SL6 7 H1
Kings Clo. SL6 8 A6
Kings Field. SL4 24 B3
Kings Gro. SL6 8 A6
Kings Rd,
 Slough. SL1 20 B6
Kings Rd,
 Windsor. SL4 25 G2
Kingstable St. SL4 22 B4
Kingswood Ct. SL6 16 B2

Kinnaird Clo. SL1 10
Kirkwall Spur. SL1 20
Knights Clo. SL4 24
Knights Pl. SL4 25
Knolton Way. SL2 21
Knowlsey Clo. SL6 7
La Roche Clo. SL3 21
Laburnham Rd. SL6 7
Laburnum Gro. SL3 26
Ladbrooke Rd. SL1 20
Ladyday Pl. SL1 19
Laggan Rd. SL6 8
Laggan Sq. SL6 8
Lake Av. SL1 20
Lake End Ct. SL6 10
Lake End Rd. SL6 18
Lakeside. SL6 8
Lake Vw. SL6 8
Lakeside Dri. SL2 12
Lambert Av. SL3 21
Lambourne Dri. SL6 15
Lammas Ct. SL4 25
Lammas Rd. SL1 10
Lancaster Av. SL2 11
Lancaster Rd. SL6 7
Lancastria Mews. SL6 7
Lancelot Clo. SL1 19
Langdale Clo. SL6 8
Langley Broom. SL3 26
Langley Park Rd. SL3 26
Langley Quay. SL3 26
Langley Rd,
 Langley. SL3 26
Langley Rd,
 Slough. SL3 21
Langton Clo. SL6 7
Langworthy End. SL6 16
Langworthy La. SL6 16
Lansdowne Av. SL1 20
Lansdowne Ct. SL1 20
Lantern Walk. SL6 8
Larch Clo. SL2 11
Larchfield Rd. SL6 15
Larkings La. SL2 13
Lascelles Rd. SL3 21
Lassell Gdns. SL6 9
Laurel Av. SL3 21
Lawkland. SL2 11
Lawn Cl. SL3 23
Lawrence Way. SL1 10
Laxton Grn. SL6 15
Layburn Cres. SL3 26
Leaholme Gdns. SL1 10
Ledgers Rd. SL1 20
Lee La. SL6 6
Leeds Rd. SL1 20
Lees Clo. SL6 15
Lees Gdns. SL4 19
Leigh Pk. SL3 23
Leigh Rd. SL1 19
Leigh Sq. SL4 24
Leighton Gdns. SL6 7
Leiston Spur. SL1 20
Leith Clo. SL1 10
Lent Green La. SL1 10
Lent Rise Rd. SL6 10
Lerwick Dri. SL1 20
Lewins Way. SL1 10
Lexington Av. SL6 15
Liddell Pl. SL4 24
Lillebrooke Cres. SL6 15
Lilley Way. SL1 18
Lime Av. SL4 22
Lime Walk. SL6 7
Linchfield Rd. SL3 23
Lincoln Ct. SL1 20
Lincoln Hatch La. SL1 10
Lincoln Rd. SL6 7
Lincoln Way. SL1 18
Linden Av. SL6 7
Linden Dri. SL2 11
Lindores Rd. SL6 16
Lingholm Clo. SL6 7
Link Rd. SL3 23
Linkswood Rd. SL1 10
Lismore Park. SL2 20
Lissett Rd. SL6 7
Litcham Spur. SL1 20
Little Buntings. SL4 24
Little Chapels Way. SL1 19
Little Sutton La. SL3 26
Littlebrook Av. SL2 19
Littledown Rd. SL1 20
Littleport Spur. SL1 20
Liverpool Rd. SL1 11
Lochinvar Clo. SL1 19
Lock Av. SL6 8

ock La. SL6 15 G2
ock Mead. SL6 8 D2
ockbridge Ct. SL6 8 D4
ocke Gdns. SL3 21 F5
ockets Clo. SL4 24 C3
oddon Dri. SL6 7 H4
oddon Spur. SL1 20 B2
odge Clo. SL1 19 H3
odge Way. SL4 24 C5
ondon Rd,
Datchet. SL3 23 E4
ondon Rd,
Langley. SL3 26 A3
ondon Rd,
Slough. SL3 21 E5
ong Dri. SL1 10 C3
ong Furlong Dri. SL2 11 E4
ong Croft. SL3 26 B2
ong Reddings La. SL2 11 G4
ongbourn. SL4 25 E5
ongleat Gdns. SL6 15 H1
ongmead. SL4 24 C3
ongworth Dri. SL6 9 E3
onsdale Clo. SL6 8 C3
onsdale Way. SL6 16 D5
oosen Dri. SL6 15 E3
oring Rd. SL4 24 D3
orne Clo. SL1 19 H4
orne Ct. SL1 19 H4
osfield Rd. SL4 24 C3
ovegrove Dri. SL2 11 E4
ovejoy La. SL4 24 B4
ovett Gdns. SL6 8 D2
owbrook Dri. SL6 15 E3
ower Boyndon Rd. SL6 7 H6
ower Britwell Rd. SL2 10 C4
ower Cippenham La.
SL1 19 E2
ower Cookham Rd.
SL6 8 D1
ower Lees Rd. SL2 11 G3
ower Peascod St. SL4 25 G3
owestoft Dri. SL1 10 C6
dlow Rd. SL6 16 A1
ff Clo. SL4 24 C5
tman La. SL6 8 B2
dford Av. SL2 12 B6
dsey Clo. SL2 11 F3
ell Rd. SL4 24 A5
nch Hill La. SL2 10 D4
nden Clo. SL6 16 D6
neham Gdns. SL6 7 F3
nton Grn. SL6 7 H5
nwood Av. SL3 21 G6

ackenzie Mall. SL1 20 C4
adeira Walk. SL4 25 H3
agnolia Gdns. SL3 21 F6
agpie Way. SL2 11 E4
aidenhead Ct Pk. SL6 8 D1
aidenhead Rd,
Dedworth. SL4 24 A2
aidenhead Rd.
Furze Platt. SL6 8 A2
ajors Farm Rd. SL3 23 G4
alders La. SL6 7 E1
allard Dri. SL1 19 F1
allow Pk. SL6 7 G3
alpas Rd. SL2 21 E3
alton Av. SL1 19 G1
alvern Rd. SL6 7 H3
anor Farm Clo. SL4 24 D5
anor House La. SL3 23 E4
anor La. SL6 16 A2
anor Rd,
Maidenhead. SL6 16 A2
anor Rd,
Windsor. SL4 24 C4
anor Way. SL6 16 C6
ansel Clo. SL2 21 E1
ansell Clo. SL4 24 C4
ansfield Clo. SL2 11 F3
aple Clo. SL6 15 G1
aple Cres. SL2 21 F3
apledurham Wk. SL6 8 A1
aplin Park. SL3 26 C1
arbeck Clo. SL4 24 B3
arcia Ct. SL1 19 E2
arescroft Rd. SL2 11 E4
arina Way. SL1 18 C1
arket La. SL3 26 D2
arket St. SL6 8 B5
arlborough Clo. SL6 7 E6
arlborough Rd,
Maidenhead. SL6 7 E6
arlborough Rd,
Slough. SL3 23 G1
arlow Rd,
Furze Platt. SL6 6 C1

Marlow Rd,
Maidenhead. SL6 8 A5
Marsh La. SL6 17 G1
Marshfield. SL3 23 F5
Martin Clo. SL6 8 A4
Martin Rd. SL1 20 B5
Martins Clo. SL4 24 B3
Martins Plain. SL2 12 C4
Marunden Grn. SL2 11 F3
Maryside. SL3 26 A1
Masons Rd. SL1 19 E1
Maybury Clo. SL1 10 C5
Mayfield Dri. SL4 25 E5
Maypole Rd. SL6 10 A5
Mead Av. SL3 26 C1
Mead Clo. SL3 26 C1
Mead Walk. SL3 26 C1
Mead Way. SL1 10 C5
Meadfield Av. SL3 26 B1
Meadfield Rd. SL3 26 B2
Meadow La. SL4 25 F1
Meadow Rd. SL3 21 H6
Meadow View La. SL6 16 A6
Meadow Way. SL6 17 G2
Meadway. SL6 8 B5
Medallion Pl. SL6 8 D5
Melbourne Av. SL1 20 A2
Mellor Wk. SL4 25 G3
Melton Ct. SL6 8 B6
Mendip Clo. SL3 26 B4
Mercia Rd. SL6 15 F2
Mercian Way. SL1 18 D2
Mere Rd. SL1 20 D6
Merlin Clo. SL3 26 C5
Merton Clo. SL6 15 G3
Merton Ct. SL1 20 D5
Merton Rd. SL. SL1 20 D5
Merwin Way. SL4 24 B5
Michael Clo. SL6 15 G1
Michaels Path. SL6 6 B3
Midcroft. SL2 11 G4
Middle Green Rd. SL3 21 H3
Middle Walk. SL1 10 B3
Middlegreen Rd. SL3 21 G5
Mildenhall Rd. SL1 20 B2
Mill La,
Maidenhead. SL6 9 E5
Mill La,
Windsor. SL4 25 E2
Mill Pl. SL3 23 G5
Mill St. SL2 20 D3
Millstream La. SL1 19 E2
Milner Rd. SL1 10 A5
Milton Rd. SL2 12 B6
Milverton Clo. SL6 15 F3
Mina Av. SL3 21 G5
Minniecroft Rd. SL1 10 B3
Minster Way. SL3 26 A1
Minton Rise. SL6 10 B6
Mirador Cres. SL2 21 E2
Missenden Gdns. SL1 10 B6
Mitchell Clo. SL1 19 G3
Moat Dri. SL2 21 F1
Moffey Hill. SL6 8 A3
Molyns Mews. SL1 18 D2
Moneycrower Dri. SL6 8 A6
Moneyrow Grn. SL6 16 C6
Monkey Island La. SL6 17 F3
Monks Rd. SL4 24 B4
Monksfield Way. SL2 11 F4
Montagu Rd,
Datchet. SL3 23 E5
Montagu Rd,
Slough. SL1 20 C3
Montem La. SL1 20 A4
Montgomery Pl. SL2 21 F2
Montpelier. SL4 25 G4
Montrose Av,
Datchet. SL3 23 F4
Montrose Av,
Slough. SL1 11 H5
Montrose Dri. SL6 7 E6
Montrose Way. SL3 23 G4
Moor End. SL6 16 D5
Moor Field Ter. SL6 8 C4
Moor Furlong. SL1 18 D2
Moor La. SL6 8 B3
Moorbridge Rd. SL6 8 C5
Moore Clo. SL1 19 G3
Moores La. SL4 19 E5
Moorlands Dri. SL6 6 D4
Moorside Clo. SL6 8 A3
Moray Dri. SL2 21 E2
Moreau Walk. SL3 21 H2
Moreland Av. SL3 26 D6
Moreland Clo. SL3 26 D6
Moreton Way. SL1 18 C2
Morley Clo. SL3 26 B1
Morrice Clo. SL3 26 B3

Mortimer Rd. SL3 21 G6
Mossy Vale. SL6 7 H3
Moundsfield Way. SL1 19 E3
Mountbatten Clo. SL1 20 D5
Mountbatten Sq. SL4 25 G3
Muddy La,
Maidenhead. SL6 7 F6
Muddy La,
Slough. SL1 20 C1
Mulberry Dri. SL3 23 H1
Mulberry Walk. SL6 7 G4
Mundesley Spur. SL1 20 B2
Murrin Rd. SL6 7 F5
Myrtle Cres. SL2 20 D2

Napier Rd. SL6 7 F6
Nash Rd. SL3 26 B3
Needham Clo. SL4 24 C3
Nelson Clo. SL3 23 G1
Nelson Rd. SL4 24 D5
Neville Clo. SL2 12 C1
New Rd, Datchet. SL3 23 G5
New Rd, Holyport. SL6 16 D6
New Rd, Langley. SL3 26 B2
New Sq. SL1 20 C4
Newberry Cres. SL4 24 B4
Newberry Way. SL1 20 B5
Newbury Dri. SL6 8 D6
Newchurch Rd. SL2 11 F5
Newhaven Spur. SL2 11 G4
Newlands Dri. SL6 7 E5
Newnham Clo. SL2 20 D4
Newport Rd. SL2 10 D4
Newton Clo. SL3 26 A1
Nicholas Gdns. SL1 18 D2
Nicholls. SL4 24 B5
Nicholsons La. SL6 8 B5
Nightingale La. SL6 7 H1
Nightingale Wk. SL4 25 G5
Nine Acres. SL1 19 F2
Nixey Clo. SL1 21 E5
Norden Clo. SL6 15 G2
Norden Rd. SL6 15 G1
Nordens Mdws. SL6 15 F1
Norelands Dri. SL1 10 B2
Norfolk Av. SL1 11 H5
Norfolk Park Cotts. SL6 8 A4
Norfolk Rd. SL6 8 A4
Norreys Dri. SL6 15 G2
North Burnham Clo.
SL1 10 B2
North Clo. SL4 24 D3
North Dean. SL6 8 B4
North Field Rd. SL6 8 B3
North Grn,
Maidenhead. SL6 8 B3
North Grn, Slough. SL1 20 C3
North Park. SL3 26 D2
North Rd. SL6 8 A5
North Star La. SL6 7 G6
North Town Clo. SL6 8 B3
North Town Mead. SL6 8 B4
North Town Moor. SL6 8 B3
North Town Rd. SL6 8 B3
Northampton Av. SL1 20 A1
Northborough Rd. SL2 11 G4
Northcroft. SL2 11 G4
Northern Rd. SL2 12 A6
Northfield Rd. SL4 19 E5
Northmead Rd. SL2 11 E4
Northumbria Rd. SL6 15 F2
Norway Dri. SL3 21 E1
Nursery La. SL3 21 G4
Nursery Rd. SL6 10 A6

Oak La. SL4 25 E3
Oak Stubbs La. SL6 17 G2
Oaken Gro. SL6 7 F4
Oakfield Av. SL1 19 G2
Oakhurst. SL6 8 D1
Oakley Cres. SL1 20 B2
Oakley Green Rd. SL4 24 A3
Oatlands Dri. SL1 20 A1
Oban Ct. SL1 20 B4
Ockwells Rd. SL6 15 F3
Odencroft Rd. SL2 11 F3
Old Court Clo. SL6 15 F3
Old Fives Ct. SL1 10 B3
Old Forge Clo. SL6 16 C3
Old Marsh La. SL6 17 G2
Old Mill La. SL6 17 E2
Oldacres. SL6 8 D5
Oldershaw Ms. SL6 7 F4
Oldfield Rd. SL6 8 C6
Oldway La. SL1 18 D3
Oldways La. SL1 18 C2
Opal Ct. SL3 13 F6
Opendale Rd. SL1 10 B5

Orchard Av,
Slough. SL1 10 C5
Orchard Av,
Windsor. SL4 25 E3
Orchard Clo. SL6 16 C3
Orchard Gro. SL6 7 G5
Orchardville. SL1 10 B4
Orwell Clo. SL4 25 G5
Osborne Ct. SL4 25 G4
Osborne Ms. SL4 25 G4
Osborne Rd. SL4 25 G4
Osborne St. SL1 20 C5
Osney Rd. SL6 8 A2
Ostlergate. SL6 7 G3
Oxford Av,
Burnham. SL1 10 A2
Oxford Av,
Slough. SL1 11 E5
Oxford Rd. SL4 25 F3
Oxford St. SL4 25 G3

Paddock Clo. SL6 15 E4
Padstow Clo. SL3 26 A1
Paget Dri. SL6 15 E2
Paget Rd. SL3 26 A3
Palace Clo. SL1 19 E2
Palmers Clo. SL6 15 E4
Palmerston Av. SL3 21 F5
Pantile Row. SL3 26 B3
Park Clo. SL4 25 H4
Park Corner. SL4 24 C5
Park Gate. SL1 10 C4
Park La. SL3 21 E6
Park Rd. SL2 12 A4
Park St,
Maidenhead. SL6 8 B5
Park St, Slough. SL1 20 D5
Park St, Windsor. SL4 25 H3
Parkland Av. SL3 23 G1
Parkside. SL6 7 H3
Parkside Walk. SL1 20 D6
Parkview Chase. SL1 10 D6
Parlaunt Rd. SL3 26 B3
Parry Grn. SL3 26 B3
Parsonage La,
Slough. SL2 12 A4
Parsonage La,
Windsor. SL4 25 E3
Parsons Wood La. SL2 12 A1
Partridge Mead. SL6 8 B2
Patricia Clo. SL1 18 D1
Paxton Av. SL1 19 H4
Pearce Clo. SL6 8 B3
Pearce Rd. SL6 8 B3
Pearl Gdns. SL1 19 G2
Pear Tree Clo. SL1 19 E2
Peascod St. SL4 25 G3
Peel Clo. SL4 25 E5
Peel Ct. SL1 11 H5
Pemberton Rd. SL2 11 E4
Penn Meadow. SL2 12 D3
Penn Rd, Datchet. SL3 23 G5
Penn Rd, Slough. SL2 12 A6
Pennine Rd. SL2 11 F5
Pennylets Grn. SL2 12 D1
Penshurst Rd. SL6 15 G1
Pentland Rd. SL2 11 F5
Penwood Ct. SL6 7 F5
Penyston Rd. SL6 7 G6
Penzance Spur. SL2 11 G4
Pepys Clo. SL3 26 C5
Percy Pl. SL3 23 F4
Perrycroft. SL4 24 C5
Perryfields Way. SL1 10 B4
Perryman Way. SL2 11 E3
Perth Av. SL1 11 G6
Peterhead Mews. SL3 26 B4
Peters La. SL6 16 D6
Petersfield Av. SL2 20 D3
Petty Pl. SL6 15 H2
Pevensey Rd. SL2 11 F5
Pheasants Croft. SL6 15 E2
Philbye Ms. SL1 19 E3
Phipps Clo. SL6 15 E4
Phipps Rd. SL1 10 D5
Pickfords Gdns. SL1 20 B3
Piece La. SL2 11 E1
Pierson Rd. SL4 24 B3
Pine Clo. SL6 7 F5
Pink La. SL1 10 A2
Pinkneys Dri. SL6 6 C5
Pinkneys Rd. SL6 7 E3
Pipers Clo. SL1 10 B2
Pitts Rd. SL1 19 H2
Plackett Way. SL1 18 D2
Plaines Clo. SL1 19 F2
Plough La. SL2 13 E3
Plough Lees La. SL1 20 C3
Plymouth Rd. SL1 11 E5

Pococks La. SL4 22 B2
Pool La. SL1 20 B3
Poolmans Rd. SL4 24 B5
Popes Clo. SL3 26 C6
Poplars Gro. SL6 8 D2
Portland Clo. SL2 10 C4
Portlock Rd. SL6 7 G5
Portsmouth Ct. SL1 20 C2
Post Office La. SL3 21 G2
Powis Clo. SL6 15 F2
Powney Rd. SL6 7 G5
Poyle La. SL1 10 A1
Preston Rd. SL2 21 F3
Prestwood. SL2 21 E2
Prince Alberts Wk. SL3 23 E5
Prince Andrew Clo. SL6 8 C4
Prince Andrew Rd. SL6 8 C4
Prince Consort Cotts.
SL4 25 G4
Princes Clo. SL4 19 E6
Princes St. SL1 21 E4
Princess Av. SL4 25 F5
Princess St. SL6 8 A6
Priors Clo,
Maidenhead. SL6 16 D4
Priors Clo,
Slough. SL1 20 D5
Priors Rd. SL4 24 B5
Priors Way. SL6 16 D4
Priory Rd. SL1 10 B5
Priory Way. SL3 23 E4
Providence Pl. SL6 8 B5
Purssell Clo. SL6 15 E3
Purton La. SL2 12 A2

Quantock Clo. SL3 26 B4
Quaves Rd. SL3 21 F5
Queen Annes Rd. SL4 25 G6
Queen Elizabeths Wk.
SL4 22 C5
Queen St. SL6 8 B6
Queen Victorias Wk.
SL4 22 C4
Queens Acre. SL4 25 G6
Queens Ct. SL1 20 D3
Queens Mead. SL3 23 E4
Queens Rd,
Datchet SL3 23 E4
Queens Rd,
Eaton Wick. SL4 19 E6
Queens Rd,
Slough. SL1 20 C3
Queens Rd,
Windsor. SL4 25 G4
Queensmere Rd 20 D4
Queensway. SL6 8 A2
Quinbrookes. SL2 21 F2

Radcot Av. SL3 26 C2
Radcot Clo. SL6 8 A2
Radnor Way. SL3 23 H1
Ragstone Rd. SL1 20 B5
Railway Ter. SL2 20 C4
Rainsborough Chase.
SL6 15 F3
Raleigh Clo. SL1 19 F2
Rambler Clo. SL6 10 B6
Rambler La. SL3 21 G6
Ramsey Ct. SL2 10 C4
Randall Clo. SL3 26 A3
Randolph Rd. SL3 21 H6
Ravensfield. SL3 21 G4
Ravensworth Rd. SL2 11 F3
Ray Dri. SL6 8 D5
Ray Lea Clo. SL6 8 C4
Ray Lea Rd. SL6 8 C3
Ray Mead Clo. SL6 8 D3
Ray Mead Rd. SL6 8 D5
Ray Meadow. SL6 8 C3
Ray Mill Rd. SL6 8 D3
Ray Mill Rd East. SL6 8 C3
Ray Mill Rd West. SL6 8 B4
Ray Park Av. SL6 8 D3
Ray Park La. SL6 8 C5
Ray Park Rd. SL6 8 C5
Ray St. SL6 8 C5
Raymond Rd,
Maidenhead. SL6 7 H5
Raymond Rd,
Slough. SL3 26 B2
Rayners Clo. SL3 26 D6
Rays Av. SL4 24 D2
Rectory Clo,
Farnham Royal. SL2 11 H2
Rectory Clo,
Windsor. SL4 25 E3
Rectory Rd. SL6 9 F3
Red Cottage Ms. SL3 21 F6
Red Ct. SL1 20 B4

Reddington Dri, Langley. SL3 26 A3
Reddington Dri, Slough. SL3 21 H6
Redford Rd. SL4 24 B3
Redriff Clo. SL6 7 H6
Redwood. SL1 10 A2
Redwood Gdns. SL1 20 A2
Reeve Rd. SL6 16 D6
Reform Rd. SL6 8 C5
Regal Ct. SL6 16 D4
Regent Ct, Slough. SL1 20 C2
Regent Ct, Windsor. SL4 25 H3
Reid Av. SL6 15 H1
Repton Clo. SL6 15 G3
Revesby Clo. SL6 15 H3
Ribstone Rd. SL6 15 F3
Richards Way. SL1 19 E2
Richmond Cres. SL1 20 D4
Rickmans La. SL2 12 C1
Ridgebank. SL1 19 F1
Riding Court Rd. SL3 23 F4
Ripley Clo. SL3 26 A2
Risborough Rd. SL6 8 A4
Riseley Rd. SL6 7 G6
River Gdns. SL6 17 E2
River Rd. SL6 9 E6
River St. SL4 25 G2
Riverside Walk. SL4 25 H2
Rixman Clo. SL6 15 H1
Rixon Clo. SL3 21 H1
Roasthill La. SL4 24 B1
Robin Hood Clo. SL1 19 E2
Rochford Way. SL6 9 H6
Rochfords Gdns. SL2 21 F3
Rockall Ct. SL3 26 C2
Roebuck Grn. SL1 18 D2
Rogers La. SL2 12 D2
Rokesby Rd. SL2 11 E2
Romney Lock Rd. SL4 25 H2
Romsey Clo. SL3 26 B2
Ronaldsay Spur. SL1 20 C1
Roseleigh Clo. SL6 7 E5
Roses La. SL4 24 C4
Rosken Gro. SL2 11 G2
Ross Rd. SL6 15 H2
Rossiter Clo. SL3 21 H6
Rowan Way. SL2 11 G5
Rowland Clo. SL4 24 B5
Rowley La. SL3 13 F2
Roxborough Way. SL6 14 D2
Roxwell Clo. SL1 19 E2
Royston Way. SL1 10 C5
Ruby Clo. SL1 19 G4
Ruddlesway. SL4 24 B3
Ruscombe Gdns. SL3 23 E3
Rushington Av. SL6 16 B1
Russel St. SL4 25 G4
Russell Ct. SL6 8 B5
Russet Rd. SL6 15 G3
Rutherford Clo. SL4 24 D3
Rutland Av. SL1 20 A1
Rutland Gate. SL6 7 G6
Rutland Pl. SL6 7 G6
Rutland Rd. SL6 7 G6
Rydings. SL4 24 C5
Rye Clo. SL6 15 E2
Ryecroft. SL4 24 D5
Rylstone Clo. SL6 15 G3
Ryvers End. SL3 26 A2
Ryvers Rd. SL3 26 A2

Sadlers Ms. SL6 8 D5
Saffron Clo. SL3 23 F5
St Adrians Clo. SL6 15 F2
St Albans St. SL4 25 H3
St Andrews Av. SL4 24 D4
St Andrews Cres. SL4 24 D5
St Andrews Way. SL1 18 D1
St Bernards Rd. SL3 21 F6
St Chads Rd. SL6 15 F2
St Cloud Way. SL6 8 B5
St Columbus Clo. SL6 15 F2
St Davids Clo. SL6 15 E2
St Elmo Clo. SL2 12 A6
St Elmo Cres. SL2 12 A6
St Georges Clo. SL4 24 C3
St Georges Cres. SL1 18 C1
St Ives Rd. SL6 8 B5
St James Pl. SL1 10 B6
St Johns Dri. SL4 25 E4
St Johns Rd, Slough. SL2 20 D3
St Johns Rd, Windsor. SL4 25 E4
St Laurence Way. SL1 20 D5
St Leonards Av. SL4 25 G4
St Leonards Hill. SL4 24 C6
St Leonards Rd. SL4 25 G4
St Lukes Rd. SL6 8 A5
St Margarets Rd. SL6 7 E5
St Marks Cres. SL6 7 F5
St Marks Pl. SL4 25 G4
St Marks Rd, Maidenhead. SL6 7 G5
St Marks Rd, Windsor. SL4 25 G4
St Marys Rd, Langley. SL3 26 A1
St Marys Rd, Slough. SL3 21 H4
St Michaels Ct. SL2 10 C4
St Patricks Clo. SL6 15 F2
St Pauls Av. SL2 20 D3
St Peters Clo. SL1 10 B4
St Peters Rd. SL6 7 H2
Salisbury Av. SL2 11 H4
Salisbury Mews. SL2 11 H4
Salt Hill Av. SL1 19 H2
Salt Hill Dri. SL1 20 A3
Salt Hill Way. SL1 20 A3
Salters Clo. SL6 8 C5
Salters Rd. SL6 8 C5
Sampsons Grn. SL2 11 F3
Sandisplatt Rd. SL6 7 E6
Sandlers End. SL2 11 G4
Sandown Rd. SL2 11 E5
Sandringham Ct. SL1 10 D6
Sandringham Rd. SL6 8 A2
Sands Farm Dri. SL1 10 C4
Sandy Mead. SL6 16 D5
Savoy Ct. SL6 8 B3
Sawyers Clo. SL4 24 C2
Sawyers Cres. SL6 15 E4
Saxon Clo,. SL3 26 A1
Saxon Gdns. SL6 9 F4
Scafell Rd. SL2 11 E4
Scarborough Way. SL1 19 G3
School La, Maidenhead. SL6 8 A3
School La, Wexham St. SL2 13 E2
School La, Slouch. SL2 20 C2
School La. SL6 14 A2
Seacourt Rd. SL3 26 C2
Second Cres. SL1 20 A1
Sefton Clo. SL2 12 D2
Sefton Paddock. SL2 13 E1
Selwyn Clo. SL4 24 C4
Severn Cres. SL3 26 C4
Seymour Clo. SL6 15 F3
Seymour Rd. SL1 20 A4
Shackleton Rd. SL1 20 C3
Shaggy Calf La. SL2 20 D2
Sharney Av. SL3 26 C2
Sheehy Way. SL2 21 F2
Sheepcote Rd, Eton Wick. SL4 19 F6
Sheepcote Rd, Windsor. SL4 24 C4
Sheephouse Rd. SL6 8 D3
Sheet St. SL4 25 H4
Sheffield Rd. SL1 20 A2
Shelley Clo. SL3 26 B4
Shenstone Dri. SL1 10 C4
Sherbourne Dri, Maidenhead. SL6 15 G3
Sherbourne Dri, Windsor. SL4 24 D6
Sherman Rd. SL1 20 C1
Sherwood Clo. SL3 21 H6
Sherwood Dri. SL6 7 E6
Shifford Cres. SL6 8 A2
Shirley Av. SL4 24 D3
Shirley Rd. SL6 15 G1
Shoppenhangers Rd. SL6 16 A2
Shoreham Rise. SL2 10 C4
Shortfern. SL2 21 F2
Sidney Rd. SL4 24 A6
Silco Dri. SL6 8 A6
Silver Clo. SL6 15 E1
Silvertrees Dri. SL6 15 E1
Simmons Clo. SL3 26 B3
Simpson Clo. SL6 8 C4
Sinclair Rd. SL4 25 G5
Slough Rd, Datchet. SL3 22 D1
Slough Rd, Eton. SL4 22 B2
Smithfield Rd. SL6 15 E3
Smiths La. SL4 24 C4
Snape Spur. SL1 20 B1
Snowball Hill. SL6 15 F6
Snowdon Clo. SL4 24 B6
Somerford Ct. SL6 8 D4
Somersby Cres. SL6 15 H3
Somerville Rd. SL4 19 H6
Sospel Ct. SL2 11 H2
South Clo. SL1 18 C1
South Field Clo. SL4 18 C4
South Grn. SL1 20 C3
South Meadow La. SL4 25 G2
South Rd. SL6 8 A6
Southcroft. SL2 11 G4
Southfield Gdns. SL1 10 B5
Southlea Rd. SL3 23 E5
Southwold Spur. SL3 26 D1
Spackmans Way. SL1 20 A6
Spencer Rd. SL3 26 A2
Spencers Clo. SL6 7 G4
Spencers Rd. SL6 7 G5
Sperling Rd. SL6 8 B3
Spinners Walk. SL4 25 G3
Spinney. SL1 19 G2
Spring Clo. SL6 8 B2
Spring Hill. SL6 16 A3
Spring La. SL1 19 F2
Springate Field. SL3 21 H5
Springfield Clo. SL4 25 F4
Springfield Pk. SL6 16 D5
Springfield Rd, Colnbrook. SL3 26 C5
Springfield Rd Windsor. SL4 25 F4
Stafferton Way. SL6 8 B6
Stafford Av. SL2 11 H4
Stafford Clo. SL6 10 B6
Stamford Rd. SL6 15 G1
Stanhope Rd. SL1 10 D6
Stanley Cotts. SL1 20 C4
Stanley Grn. SL3 26 A3
Stanton Way. SL3 23 H1
Starwood Ct. SL3 21 F5
Station App. SL6 8 B6
Station Rd, Cippenham. SL1 10 D6
Station Rd, Langley. SL3 26 B2
Station Rd, Maidenhead. SL6 9 H5
Staunton Rd. SL2 12 B6
Stephenson Dri. SL4 25 E2
Stewart Av. SL1 20 C1
Stile Rd. SL3 21 G6
Stirling Clo. SL4 24 B4
Stirling Gro. SL6 7 E4
Stirling Rd. SL1 11 F5
Stockdales Rd. SL4 19 E5
Stockwells. SL6 9 F3
Stoke Court Dri. SL2 12 C3
Stoke Gdns. SL1 20 C3
Stoke Grn. SL2 12 D5
Stoke Park Av. SL2 11 H3
Stoke Poges La, Slough. SL1 20 B4
Stoke Poges La, Stoke Poges. SL2 12 C6
Stoke Rd. SL2 20 C4
Stokesay. SL2 20 D2
Stomp Rd. SL1 10 B5
Stompits Rd. SL6 16 D6
Stonebridge Field. SL4 19 H6
Stonefield Pk. SL6 7 G5
Stoney La. SL2 11 G1
Stoney Meade. SL1 19 G2
Stornoway Rd. SL3 26 D3
Stour Clo. SL1 19 G4
Stovell Rd. SL4 25 F2
Stowe Rd. SL1 19 E1
Stranraer Gdns. SL1 20 C4
Stratfield Rd. SL1 20 D4
Stratford Clo. SL2 10 D4
Stratford Gdns. SL6 15 G3
Streamside. SL1 19 E2
Stroma Ct. SL1 18 D1
Stroud Clo. SL4 24 B5
Stroud Farm Rd. SL6 16 D6
Stuart Clo. SL4 24 D4
Stuart Way. SL4 24 C4
Sturt Grn. SL6 16 A6
Suffolk Clo. SL1 10 D6
Suffolk Rd. SL6 15 H2
Sumburgh Spur. SL1 20 B1
Summerlea. SL1 19 G2
Summerleaze Rd. SL6 8 C3
Summers Rd. SL1 10 B3
Sun Clo. SL4 22 A3
Sun La. SL6 8 A5
Sunbury Rd. SL4 22 B3
Sunderland Rd. SL6 7 F4
Surly Hall Clo. SL4 24 D3
Surrey Av. SL2 11 H4
Sussex Clo. SL1 21 E5
Sussex Pl. SL1 21 E5
Sutton Av. SL3 21 F5
Sutton Clo. SL6 15 D1
Sutton La. SL3 26 C5
Sutton Pl. SL3 26 C5
Swabey Rd. SL3 26 B3
Switchback Clo. SL6 7 H2
Switchback Rd. SL6 7 H1
Switchback Rd Nth. SL6 7 H2
Switchback Rd Sth. SL6 7 H2
Sycamore Clo. SL6 15 F3
Sycamore Ct. SL4 25 G5
Sycamore Walk. SL3 21 H2
Sydney Gro. SL1 20 A2
Sykes Rd. SL1 11 G5
Sylvester Rd. SL6 8 A2

Talbot Av. SL3 26 A1
Talbot Pl. SL3 23 G5
Talbots Dri. SL6 7 E6
Tamar Way. SL3 26 C3
Tamarisk Way. SL1 19 G2
Tangier Ct. SL4 22 B3
Tangier La. SL4 22 B3
Taplow Common Rd. SL1 10 A1
Taplow Rd. SL6 10 A5
Tarbay La. SL4 24 A4
Tatchbrook Clo. SL6 8 B4
Tavistock Clo. SL6 7 E5
Taylors Ct. SL6 7 F4
Teesdale Rd. SL2 11 F5
Telford Dri. SL1 19 G2
Temple Rd. SL4 25 G4
Tennyson Way. SL2 10 D4
Testwood Rd. SL4 24 B3
Thames Av. SL4 25 H2
Thames Cres. SL6 8 D2
Thames Mead. SL4 24 C3
Thames Rd. SL3 26 C3
Thames St. SL4 25 H2
Thameside. SL4 25 H2
Thatchers Dri. SL6 15 E1
The Avenue, Datchet. SL3 23 E5
The Avenue, Maidenhead. SL6 8 D2
The Binghams. SL6 16 C3
The Briars. SL3 26 A4
The Cedars. SL2 11 E3
The Chase. SL6 7 H2
The Cherries. SL2 21 F2
The Close. SL1 18 C1
The Conifers. SL6 7 E4
The Courtyards. SL3 26 B1
The Crescent, Maidenhead. SL6 8 A5
The Crescent, Slough. SL1 20 B5
The Croft. SL6 15 G1
The Dell. SL6 15 E4
The Drive, Datchet. SL3 23 F5
The Drive, Slough. SL3 21 H5
The Fairway, Burnham. SL1 10 C3
The Fairway, Maidenhead. SL6 15 F3
The Farthingales. SL6 8 D5
The Frithe. SL2 21 E2
The Glen. SL3 21 G6
The Gore. SL6 9 H2
The Green, Burnham. SL1 10 B4
The Green, Datchet. SL3 23 E4
The Green, Slough. SL1 20 A5
The Greenway. SL1 18 D2
The Grove. SL1 20 D5
The Hatch. SL4 24 A2
The Link. SL2 21 F2
The Limes. SL4 14 A4
The Long Walk. SL4 25 H5
The Myrke. SL4 22 D1
The Normans. SL2 21 E1
The Paddock, Datchet. SL3 23 E5
The Paddock, Maidenhead. SL6 7 G3
The Pagoda. SL6 8 D3
The Parade. SL4 24 B3
The Points. SL6 15 F3
The Pound. SL1 10 C4
The Precincts. SL1 10 B4
The Redwoods. SL4 25 G5
The Ridings. SL6 7 E6
The Rushes. SL6 8 D6
The Spur. SL1 10 D5
The Terrace. SL6 17 E3
The Tressel. SL6 15 G
The Walk. SL4 19 F
The Went. SL3 26 D
The Wheatbutts. SL4 19 F
The Wicketts. SL6 7 G
Thicket Gro. SL6 6 D
Third Cres. SL1 20 A
Thirkelby Clo. SL1 19 H
Thirlmere Av. SL1 10 E
Thomas Ct. SL6 15 F
Thompson Clo. SL3 26 E
Thorn Dri. SL3 21 H
Thorndike. SL2 11 C
Thrift La. SL6 15 C
Thurlby Way. SL6 15 H
Thurston Rd. SL1 20 E
Tilbury Wk. SL3 26 C
Tilstone Av. SL4 19 E
Tilstone Clo. SL4 19 E
Timbers Walk. SL6 15
Tinkers La. SL4 24 E
Tintern Clo. SL1 19 H
Tithe Barn Dri. SL6 17
Tithe Clo. SL6 16 D
Tithe Ct. SL3 26
Tockley Rd. SL1 10
Tollgate. SL6 7
Tomlin Rd. SL2 11
Topaz Clo. SL1 19
Torquay Spur. SL2 11
Torridge Rd. SL3 26
Travic Rd. SL2 11
Travis Ct. SL2 11
Treesmill Dri. SL6 15
Trelawney Av, Langley. SL3 26
Trelawney Av, Slough. SL3 21
Trenchard Rd. SL6 16
Trent Rd. SL3 26
Trinity Pl. SL4 25
Troutbeck Clo. SL2 20
Trumper Way. SL1 19
Truro Clo. SL6 7
Tubwell Rd. SL2 13
Tudor Ct. SL6 8
Tudor Gdns. SL1 10
Tudor Way. SL4 24
Tunis La. SL1 20
Turner Rd. SL3 21
Turnoak Pk. SL3 24
Turpins Grn. SL6 15
Turton Way. SL1 20
Tweed Rd. SL3 26
Twinches La. SL1 19
Two Mile Dri. SL 18
Twynham Rd. SL6 7
Tyrrell Gdns. SL4 24

Ullswater Clo. SL1 10
Umberville Way. SL2 11
Underhill Clo. SL6 7
Upcroft. SL4 25
Upper Bray Rd. SL6 16
Upper Lees Rd. SL2 11
Upton Clo. SL1 20
Upton Court Rd. SL3 20
Upton Pk. SL1 20
Upton Rd. SL1 20
Uxbridge Rd. SL1 21

Vale Gro. SL1 20
Vale Rd. SL4 24
Valley End. SL3 13
Vansittart Rd. SL4 25
Vantage Rd. SL1 19
Vanwall Rd. SL6 15
Vaughan Gdns. SL4 19
Vermont Rd. SL2 11
Verney Rd. SL3 26
Vicarage Dri. SL6 16
Vicarage Pl. SL1 21
Vicarage Rd. SL6 8
Vicarage Walk. SL6 16
Vicarage Way. SL3 26
Victor Clo. SL6 7
Victor Rd. SL6 25
Victoria Rd, Eton Wick. SL4 19
Victoria Rd, Slough. SL2 21
Victoria St, Slough. SL1 20
Victoria St, Windsor. SL4 25
Village Rd. SL4 18
Villiers Rd. SL2 12

Wade Dri. SL1 19